Praise for The 4 Money Mindsets

"This deeply caring book is about so much more than money. The lessons it contains to help anybody manage their relationship with money are rooted in the author's lifelong drive to understand the reasons for the vast differences in wealth and happiness in her own family

Down to earth and unflinching, *The 4 Money Mindsets* is at times an uncomfortable read - but that's precisely because it takes away excuses and offers a pathway for anyone who isn't where they want to be financially.

As a 'self-taught' serial entrepreneur, I saw the detailed reasons for my success and I identified what I am not so good at. Wherever you are financially - debt-ridden, just getting by, or well off - this book will change your life for the better."

Phil Morse, DJ, author, founder of *DigitalDJTips.com*

"I really love this book! It is practical and up there with the best, combining real life stories with practical step-by-step exercises that show you how to shift your money mindset.

There is gold here. This book has inspired me and changed my relationship with money. My first thought was 'instant grab'."

Jill Saville, Executive and Leadership Coach, Trainer and Speaker, Founding partner *John Maxwell Team.*

"This is a must-read for anyone serious about building wealth with powerful perspectives on leverage; the money mindsets and how to shift them; detailed matrices on time and money planning. This is an essential read for those stuck in a rut with business or personal finances."

Mark Chimley, Cyber Security specialist, entrepreneur and Co-Founder of *Genus One.*

"I absolutely love this book. It's the financial education that I needed and believe should be widely accessible in schools! At its core, the journey represents a deeper relationship with the self. The tools and exercises relate to money but can be applied to other areas of our lives.

Karen's passion for this subject is obvious and she's created an engaging book around a touchy subject."

Kevin Wilkinson, CEO
New Dawn Investment Group Ltd.

"This is a book I've been waiting for! If you want to understand your deep-seated beliefs about money then this is the book to read! The author skilfully mixes theory, practical exercises and her own extensive experience to challenge your money 'mindset' and help you to see money as a tool no matter how much or little you have. A thoroughly fascinating and engaging read! "

Isabel Frenzel, senior government employee

"Thanks to *The 4 Money Mindsets* I have been able to understand how my money mindset has held me back and the barriers that are stopping me moving forward."

Judy Parsons, Author, entrepreneur, *LinkedIn* specialist

"I read this book from cover to cover in a day. It is brimming with insights, life stories and knowledge and enthuses you with a sense of certainty that you can change your money mindset through following the practical advice and steps that are provided throughout the book. It's left me feeling excited about the future that I can achieve."

Rachael Pinks, Artist, Curator & Business Owner

"The 4 Money Mindsets is a powerful insight into your underlying beliefs and attitudes about money. Not only will it help you understand your current mindset it will advise and inspire you how to change that mindset in line with your long term goals and dreams.

This is a must read for anyone who is not happy with their current financial situation. Without changing your mindset you won't change your financial situation.

Just a few days after reading *The 4 Money Mindsets* I saw real positive change in my life and future financial prospects. I never realised my mindset was holding me back so much or the power a few changes to my mindset could have on my life. This is the ideal book for anyone not happy with their financial situation.

By the end of the book I was truly inspired and had a plan laid out before me on how to change my mindset."

Paul Bassi, Author, Entrepreneur & Founder
of *Web Design Myna*

"Thank you, thank you, thank you Karen for making sense of my relationship with money in your fabulous, warm, genuine and thought-provoking way.

The 4 Money Mindsets has made a huge difference to my life to the point where I have stopped accumulating debt. Thank you for helping me understand and believe I could make the changes needed to make a real difference.

Understanding your relationship with money makes a huge difference to your life, your business, your relationships and your health. If you want a wealthier life, then you owe it to yourself to read this book and take action.

Katy Henry, Director, *The Bridge Centre for Natural Health*

"This is a book about relationships. *The 4 Money Mindsets* has taken me on a journey allowing me to revisit transactions with others - and with money - throughout my life. It allowed me to revisit my own attitudes towards money, and the unseen but very real barriers that literally limit progress.

The 4 Money Mindsets helps you explore your relationship with money: earning it, losing it, keeping it, managing it and growing it. "

Helen Myrie, Career Coach, Nottingham UK.

"Love this book. Loved travelling the exciting journey towards transformation! I am eternally grateful for the real possibilities already showing up in my life, simply from exploring this thoroughly interesting and insightful read. Who could have guessed finance could be so understandable and doable for us all.

From the beginning, I felt accompanied by a top expert in the field; guiding, clarifying, gently encouraging me through my own financial 'stuff', pointing out the next steps to financial freedom and future success. The deeper I went into it, the lighter I felt.

I take my hat off to Karen Sutton-Johal in celebration of all the gifts passionately shared in *The 4 Money Mindsets*: gifts I can't wait to share, recommend, and pay forward.

Laura Clifton, Author and facilitator, UK

"This is a smart, inspired and practical book full of insights and exercises that adds depth to the topic of money management and wealth creation."

Andrew Priestley, Business coach,
Author *The Money Chimp*.

THE 4 MONEY
MINDSETS

KAREN SUTTON-JOHAL

WRITING MATTERS PUBLISHING

The 4 Money Mindsets
Karen Sutton-Johal

First published in 2016

Writing Matters Publishing
Kent UK

info@writingmatterspublishing.com
www.writingmatterspublishing.com

ISBN 978-0-9575440-9-3 (pbk)

A CIP catalogue record for this book is available from the British Library.

This book is available to order online from Amazon and Kindle.

Please note: The 4 Money Mindsets is intended as information only and does not constitute specific financial, investment, taxation or legal advice unique to your situation. It is for educational purposes only. The sole aim is to help the reader better understand the four money mindsets. The Author, Publisher and Resellers accept no responsibility for loss, damage or injury to persons or their belongings as a direct or indirect result of reading this book.

Dedication

This book is dedicated to anyone who worries about not having enough money and lies awake at night thinking about how they are going to get the money they need, now or in the future.

It's for anyone who feels trapped by their financial situation and doesn't understand what to do or how to make better financial decisions.

It's for those who want a plan and strategies to ensure they always have enough money to live life as they choose.

This book is especially for anyone with the courage to change and become the person they were meant to be.

Contents

The 4 Money Mindsets at a glance

Extensive review

The 4 Money Mindsets is the result of years of experience as a debt advisor and a coach working with clients with money worries; an extensive review of client histories; and a broad review of money management books, websites and courses.

The 4 Money Mindsets

An extensive long-term review has identified four key money mindsets - *In-Debt, Break-Even, Comfortable* and *Rich*.

People have or don't have money depending on one of four mindsets. Essentially, people with a debt mindset typically end up back in debt even if they are repeatedly assisted to become debt-free. And people who have a Rich mindset will always find a way to become rich, even if they lose all their money and have to start all over again.

How You Will Benefit

The 4 Money Mindsets is designed to help you identify and better understand your money mindset; and to provide strategies for changing your money mindset if it needs to change.

You need to approach this material with an open mind because it will positively challenge the way you think, feel and behave with money. To benefit most, do the activities as designed. The ultimate message of this book is to take on *conscious* accountability for a positive relationship with money.

Road-tested on Clients Over Many Years

All material in this book has been road-tested with actual clients over many years in the professional capacity as a qualified debt advisor and money coach.

*The 4 Money Mindset*s only includes strategies that work. That said, this book does not replace the input of a qualified debt advisor or money coach but you will still find the practical exercises most useful if you complete the activities as suggested.

If you have chronic money worries you need to seek professional help from a qualified debt counsellor.

If you have a serious debt problem don't stick your head in the sand. Contact *Step Change Debt Charity* who provide free advice nationwide to anyone on freecall, 0800 138 1111. Time and again they have provided amazing support and advice to anyone I have referred there.

Online Resources

You can access a broad range of useful resources at:

www.the4moneymindsets.com

Part 1

Origins of the
4 Money Mindsets

Introduction

How Money Really Works

"If you're born poor, it's not your mistake.
But if you die poor, it is your mistake."

Bill Gates

Very few people go through life without some unfulfilled hopes, aspirations and dreams. Most of us wish for better and spend a lifetime striving, often working long and hard. To add to this, life throws some choice curve balls – divorce, illness, bankruptcy or worse – to knock us out.

A few seem to have it sussed, always landing on their feet, getting rich easily. The majority, though, just grind on day in day out, barely able to pay the bills, sometimes slipping in and out of debt depending on what's going on for them. Never seeming to find peace with money, they spend their lives doing whatever they can to ensure they have enough to carry on.

Many of us feel that if we just had more money, everything would be OK; yet we feel completely powerless to control how we acquire money or hold on to it.

I have spent much of my life analysing what people do with their money and the effects of this in their lives.

My dad grew up in an extremely wealthy family. My mother grew up in a very poor family and married my father for his family's wealth – not because she was a heartless gold digger but because she believed that the only way for a poor person like her to become rich would be to find someone who was already wealthy to share that wealth with her.

My dad's family was hugely disapproving of their marriage and, rather than sharing their wealth, expected my parents to be responsible for themselves. For a time, my parents were penniless.

For years I watched what my parents and their relatives, both rich and poor, did with their money, and the effect this had not just on their own lives but also on the lives of those around them. It taught me a lot.

I saw from the people around me that whether you end up wealthy or in poverty is a choice. As you will discover, it all depends on how you think and then act with money.

Preface

My Story

Throughout my life I have been obsessed with understanding how some people always manage to have lots of money while so many others never seem to have any.

When I was about six years old, I was hiding in the corner, listening and watching my parents as everything for them fell apart.

My father's business had collapsed and they were financially destroyed. Our phone had been cut off and the electricity would go in a couple of days. The bank manager had been to my father's parents' house to inform them that if they did not help with their son's huge debts, the bank would take our house. This was particularly painful because my grandparents had disapproved immensely of my parents' marriage and there was no certainty that they would help.

Later that day, I sat in the car next to my mother as she drove from place to place, crying with despair and shame while trying to sell little packets of hair accessories – all to no avail. She cried and cried. I felt very sad and very scared.

At the time I didn't appreciate that I was beginning to form a lifelong emotional connection with money.

Unconsciously, deep down, I vowed there and then to always have enough money. I would never sit beside my terrified child, crying, without a penny to my name.

And so began my life's work: to understand how those who always had enough money got it and kept it; and to replicate this in my own life.

I learned how people with very little money often stayed that way regardless of how much came into their lives. And how those with very little money can accumulate wealth.

I have worked as a debt adviser, a skills specialist and business coach. I have also built a property business, all of which have given me insights into people's successes and failures with money, but more importantly their mindset.

I began by observing and questioning the people around me. I aimed to find out how much money they had, how they got it and what they did with it.

I asked everyone I could about their thoughts on why some had lots of money, and so very many others almost none. Over the years, bit by bit I pursued my interest relentlessly, and soon I started to see a distinct pattern: *how much money you have or don't have depends on your mindset.* And I identified four key mindsets.

My own family background provided me with plenty of clear examples of financial success and failure. Yours might too. My father had come from what was then one of the richest families in Ireland, while my mother hailed from an extremely poor background.

Here's what I discovered.

My Family History

My mother grew up as the daughter of a wood turner in the abject poverty of 1940's Ireland.

During my childhood, I spent endless hours talking to my maternal grandmother about her past, and it was from her that I developed a deep interest in history.

Granny's life experiences helped me see the world in a different way, through learning to understand people and the circumstances in which they found themselves. Her grandparents and parents had both survived the 'Great Hunger', the Irish Potato Famine of 1848.

I vividly remember her telling me a tale about her home town of Kilcommon in County Tipperary. During the famine, her family was boiling maize in a big pot on the fire. A starving man forced himself in through the window, thrust his hands straight into the boiling pot and began to devour the food. He scalded himself fatally; his hands, mouth and throat burnt out and he screamed and howled in agony. Despite their best efforts to help he died of his injuries in their home.

Granny lived through two World Wars and a Civil War in Ireland, and was a committed socialist. I was enthralled by the story of her being arrested in 1918 for protesting on the O'Connell Bridge in Dublin.

Granny believed that money was generated from the sweat on the backs of the working man and woman – and that the rich were parasites on the poor.

She believed that any ordinary person who managed to feed themselves and their children was good with money.

Granny did not have a bank account because she thought they were the instruments of the rich (and the devil). She also feared they might someday close the bank and keep her money.

Her household expenses were managed with three jars – one for bills, one for food and one put aside for other expenses.

She believed that rich people were rich because they had taken from the poor and that they were immoral scoundrels. The words she used to describe my father's family are unprintable!

She believed in scripture, *Blessed are the poor*. She felt that the poor people – those with little in the way of money - gave their all, often dying from working down mines, building or toiling in the fields to make the rich richer who gave them no more than the scrapings from their table.

Coming from a very different environment, Dad's family had gardeners and maids and still paid an allowance to Josephine, an elderly, retired family nanny. Dad often told us that his family members were the only ones, besides the ambulance in Cork, with enough petrol to run a car during WW2.

I grew up in Cork literally surrounded by icons of my father's family history of wealth and power. Suttons Coals, a large coal merchant business of which my paternal grandfather was Chairman, had been an established name in Cork for 150 years. Sutton House, the large headquarters building, stood in the South Mall, the financial district of Cork.

I remember regularly watching the St. Patricks Day Parade with my siblings from the top floor. Family days out with my grandparents involved sailing on their yacht and dinner at the yacht club, where I sat riveted by their conversations with friends. From a young age, I observed that they spoke about very different subjects than my maternal grandparents.

I used to ask my paternal grandmother, Eileen Roche, to tell me over and over again how her father, William Roche, founded Roches Stores. William dreamed of setting up a shop that would sell household goods to ordinary people at reasonable prices. Until then, shopping in this way had only been an option open to the rich.

William worked relentlessly to achieve his vision. Before striking out on his own, he worked for *Cash & Co* in Cork for nine years, saving every penny he could to fund his business.

His first shop failed, and so did the second. His third shop, Roches Stores, was a huge success and developed into a chain of department stores throughout Ireland. The Cork branch, a magnificent building, was situated in the best location on the main street, and was Cork's answer to Selfridges on Oxford Street in London. While building the business, however, he slept under the escalator on a straw mattress, his rationale being that because it was so uncomfortable it would force him out of bed at 5am every morning to get on with the day's work.

My Grandfather's uncle, Sir Abraham Sutton, was High Sheriff and later Lord Mayor of Cork. His house was close to the one I grew up in and has now been converted into an opulent hotel. I remember returning one evening with Dad and his friend to the yacht club to moor our fishing boat, and Dad's uncle Stanley Roche's yacht was tied up next to the then Irish Prime Minister's yacht. Stanley's yacht was bigger!

Interestingly, my father was adamant that the Roche branch of the family were not very respectable compared with the Suttons. My father believed that the Suttons had been in business for over 200 years whereas the Roches had only been in business for about 70 years.

The Sutton side of my father's family strongly disagreed with my parents' marriage. I came to believe that such disapproval of marriages was almost mandatory as many of my relatives seemed at one time or another to be a target. When my father's parents (Eric Sutton and Eileen Roche) married, that marriage too had met with disapproval.

Eric Sutton's mother (Maud Healey) was horrified and refused to visit their house. *A Sutton married to a Roche? Oh my God!* The Roches were (horror of horrors) *'new money'*.

Going back further, when Maud married Braham Sutton, her family was so disgusted that she had stooped to marry *'trade'* that (the story goes) her family disowned her. Neither of my grandparents would speak about it so I was never able to get any details from them.

Growing up with such contrasts within the family was a opportunity to immerse myself in a diverse range of attitudes and behaviours towards people with and without money.

In particular, I found the snobbery about *'new money'* and class fascinating. My father, grandparents, aunts and uncles had got themselves in such a flap! These marriages had involved one party with a title or the social status of *'old money'* (which was in fact running out) walking down the aisle with a *'new money'* partner seeking the respectability of the *'old money'*. From my young perspective, it seemed that *'old money'* meant broke, while *'new money'* actually had the cash.

The Immediate Family Influence

My mother believed marrying into a wealth family would automatically mean she became wealthy herself. She didn't understand that it didn't work like that at all; she never became wealthy and never appreciated why. She just thought that her in-laws were vicious, mean people who were unwilling to pass some of their excess wealth on to her and my father.

My mother had no understanding of the money game. She had never been brought up to understand that in every market there are buyers and sellers; that people who become wealthy add value and are financially rewarded in return. That's the name of the game; that's how it works.

In my father's family, *'old money'* was *'selling'* social status and respectability, which is why *'new money'* was willing to buy. Thus money was shared and continued to flow. In that sense, my mother didn't have any *'value'* to add to the Suttons or the Roches.

She spent her married life vacillating between obsequiousness and hatred towards them, depending on whether they were inclined to give our family any money or not.

Having been brought up in a poor household, she had only seen examples of rich people at the cinema or in magazines.

She thought that the only way for someone like her to become rich would be through someone else giving her money. She never understood that she could have chosen to create her own wealth, but believed that attaining wealth was a matter of luck, like a lottery win, windfall, gift or contribution in her favour. She never understood that to become wealthy in her own right, she would have to develop a system to create it.

My father worked for a wage for his own father in Suttons – a business that my grandfather had inherited – but soon discovered that he had no influence in how that business was run. In a fit of pique, after failing to persuade his father to introduce a change into the business, he left and set up on his own.

The period following the failure of my father's business was a terrible time in our lives. My father buried his head in the sand and went fishing for eighteen months; my mother took me, my brother and sister and the family cat to live with her parents in another city, where she retrained as a teacher so she could work to support the family.

For the next two years the four of us (and the cat) lived in a tiny house with my grandparents, my aunt and her two children. I have a clear recollection of fighting with my cousin over a piece of meat. Five of us shared a bedroom. When my little brother was born he had to be cared for by someone outside of the family because we did not have the space, or Mum the time, to have him with us. I learned some very valuable lessons from this experience. You can endure very harsh living conditions and still survive.

The experience also meant that I was more exposed to how other people behaved with money.

My mother's sister (the aunt with whom we shared the house) was a single parent and permanently mired in debt. Although she had a well-paid job she would spend and spend.

She was miserable when in trouble because of her debts, which was most of the time. If somebody bailed her out by way of help from the family, consolidation loans or through other means she would simply get into more debt.

A bad 'pay your debts or else' letter would arrive – and she would cope with the stress by going on holiday (using borrowed money), convinced that 'she deserved it' because of the stress caused by the debt.

I used to shake my head in wonder. I realised that giving her more money would not solve the problem; it would in fact make it worse. She appeared to be in a self-destructive mental pattern.

These experiences taught me about different people and their different beliefs and behaviours around money.

I went from a private school in Cork where people spoke English to a state school in Limerick where only Irish was spoken.

I learned a great deal at that school, including how to get on with people from all backgrounds. Few of the kids in this school came from wealthy backgrounds and I could see that their parents' mindsets were very different to the mindsets of the parents at my previous private school.

Two years later, my mother, now with four children, returned to the family home in Cork, where she got a job as a school teacher and worked until she retired around thirty years later.

A broken man, my father went to work for Roches Stores in a job he loathed with every fibre of his being. He continued to work there for the remainder of his working life, forcing himself to go in every day because he feared he would not be able to claim his company pension if he retired early.

My parents ground on for the rest of their lives hating their jobs, hating the unjust taxation system and never seeming to get ahead. They were taxed so highly that we remained poor even when they both had reasonably good jobs. When the exhaust pipe on Dad's car broke, he tied it up with string because we could not afford to have it mended. The phone was regularly disconnected because we could not pay the bill; the man from the electricity company regularly turned up to disconnect our electricity. Mum had to choose between dental care for herself and university fees for us. She let her teeth rot.

Because of these experiences, both my parents bitterly resented anyone with their own business or anyone on benefits.

They felt people with businesses could avoid the crippling taxes they had to endure in 1980's Ireland.

Two of my uncles on my father's side ran businesses, and my parents thought life was so much easier for them. However, I remember both uncles almost losing their homes on more than one occasion, and they had several business failures between them – five or six that I can remember!

Instead of giving up they got up and started another business until they were successful, and they did eventually become very successful. They had a terrible time when things went wrong but did not get as completely crushed as my Dad did. They were resilient.

My parents resented those on benefits, and held the opinion that they were supporting such people by paying taxes and going without themselves while benefit recipients received so much more. I recall my parents feeling betrayed because, whilst both of them worked, none of us could have eye tests, glasses or dental treatment; people on benefits, however, could easily get treatment for free.

At the age of 63, my father had a massive panic attack and was unable to work again. His uncle, who owned the business, arranged for him to retire with his pension but his health was destroyed. He was barely able to walk and remained in constant pain.

This time of life should have been a fairy tale ending to a very tough journey for my parents. But it ended tragically.

In the early 2000s, Dad spotted that Anglo Irish Bank shares were set to rise. He bought 72,000 shares over the next three to four years, which at their height were worth over €17 per share.

My mother, myself and one of my siblings also had large holdings of these shares.

My abiding memory of my father is of him sitting in front of the television, scrolling Bloomberg TV hour after hour, year after year, watching the Anglo Irish Bank share price.

I sold my shares in the summer of 2006 against my father's advice, because I needed to fund a business that would provide my family with immediate cash flow. My father and sibling held complete faith that the shares would keep on rising and rising.

On 2nd September 2007, he told me they would double in price over the coming two years. Dad died five days later.

My mother and siblings 'held their nerve' and kept their holdings while my father's estate went through probate. But on 15th January 2009, the Anglo Irish Bank was nationalised and they lost everything. None of them ever enjoyed any of the good things the money could have done for them. It was as if they were destined not to be rich, even though the wealth was theirs for the taking. Years later my mother was still in shock.

My Quest

My family experience around money was terrible. But I knew there had to be more to it than simple bad luck. What made some people always come up trumps and end up wealthy while others never made it? How did some manage to become rich again even after losing everything? Why did others seem destined to struggle forever, no matter how much money came their way?

I recognised that there was some kind of pattern going on that caused it to happen. I had seen different people approach the same events in different ways and get different results. So was it the approach that accounted for these differing results?

Untangling this became, for me, an all-consuming goal. After working as a debt advisor my conclusion is your money mindset makes all the difference.

And I discovered four money mindsets.

Chapter 1
What is Financial Success?

How Money Really Works

On my journey of discovery I knew that if I could unravel how money really works, I would have control to live the life I wanted.

I dug around for years unpicking every opinion on the subject so that I could gain an understanding. I got so many versions from different groups of people, each of whom were vehement that they understood how money worked. Eventually it became clear that each had an important piece of the puzzle but not the whole picture.

So what is Financial Success?

The typical belief is that financial success equates to beautiful people with big houses, holidays, cars and bling.

My work as a debt adviser showed me that external appearances can be very deceptive. I visited many families with big houses, flashy cars, big televisions all the external trappings who were deeply in debt. Tragically, they were on the brink of losing everything.

When I was very young and with my father, I clearly remember a woman saying to him, "I saw your uncle, Stanley Roche, the other day, and he was dressed so poorly you would give him tuppence" meaning that to her, he looked as poor as a beggar. My dad laughed and said, "When you are genuinely rich, you don't need to prove it to anyone."

I now know that overt exhibitions of wealth aren't necessarily real indicators of wealth. I wanted to find out what 'financial success' really meant. To do that, I used my expertise in capability analysis to identify what exactly makes someone financially successful.

Is there a Universal Definition?

I have coached and interviewed hundreds of people, some rich, some very poor, and a great many in between. I always ask my clients a number of specific questions:

1. What is money?
2. How do you get your money?
3. What do you do with it once you get it?
4. If you need more money how do you get it?
5. What would someone who is good with money do with it once they get it?
6. How do rich people get rich?
7. How do poor people become poor?

The answers to these questions almost always result in four groups sharing four separate and distinct perspectives of financial success. Interestingly, each person is adamant that their perspective is right.

Group 1 - There's never enough money

The first group feels that no matter what they do, there is simply never enough money.

"As soon as I get my money some or most of it is gone! It goes to pay debts, then I buy what I need."

"I get money from my job, pension, welfare or relative, and I do not have much control over how much I get. I take what I am given."

"If I needed more money I would have to borrow it."

This group of people acknowledge that financially successful people have the ability to spend wisely and not waste money. But they usually feel that rich people are very lucky, dishonest, mean or even a combination of all these.

And they believe that the poor are poor because they lack enough money. Some believe they don't have enough because others have taken more than their fair share.

Group 2 - Debt is bad (and should be avoided)

The second group also feels that financially successful people are good at managing money, but they believe strongly debt is bad, and that people should learn to manage on what they have (now).

"Someone who is good with money always pays their bills and is *never* in debt. If they have enough left over any payment period, they should save for something specific."

"I receive money from my job, pension, welfare or relative, and I do not have much control over how much I get."

"I take what I'm given and have to manage on that. If I wanted more money I would have to work more hours and work harder."

They feel that saving in itself - other than for a specific purchase such as a holiday - is almost impossible. But there is usually never enough left over. They feel the rich are lucky or even dishonest. People are poor because they spend more than they earn. But they don't earn enough.

Group 3 - Don't waste money!

The third group feels completely responsible for their financial security. In their view, financially successful people make sure they save for a rainy day.

"Someone who is good with money will always save a proportion first and then live on the rest."

This group are very good at spotting financial risks. They believe people with debts are feckless and wasteful. They resent people who run up debts and then need help. They regard them as undeserving.

"I get money from my job, pension, welfare or relative, and I do not have much control over how much I get. I take what I am given."

"If I wanted more money I would have to work more hours, and harder. I do, however, have great control over what I save and spend. When I get money I save a proportion and spend the rest."

They believe the rich become rich through luck, dishonesty, risk-taking – often excessive risk-taking – and (to a lesser extent) hard work.

Group 4 - Money comes from value adding assets

The fourth group feel entirely responsible for their financial success, admire wealthy people and seek to emulate them.

"I get my money from my assets."

"Someone who is good with money
would leverage money to create more."

"If I want more money I need to figure out how to add value
or create more assets that will generate more money."

They think some rich people are lucky, although many say *you make your own luck*. They believe those who do not take responsibility for their financial success or leave it to others will never be rich, and to some extent deserve to be poor.

Which one sounds the most like you?

In addition to the four groups are three financial themes:

- Financial success is the result of specific sets of skills.
- We learn (or don't learn) about financial success.
- Financial success (attitudes and behaviours) is modelled from the people around us.

Financial Success and Specific Skills

Financial success is underpinned by five key financial skill sets:

- **Creating money** - building a successful business, inventing and bringing to market a successful product, creating a successful investment strategy.
- **Saving money** - being able to amass large savings regardless of income.
- **Managing money** - skillful budgeting and an ability to stretch scarce resources (the sort of person who can create a delicious meal from an apparently empty fridge).
- **Spending money** - spending money wisely to improve one's life, being able to make the right (prudent) purchasing decisions for the right price at the right time.
- **Giving money** - knowing when to give, to whom, for what, and how much is the key.

How We Learn about Finance

There are two key themes.

We are not taught financial success at school

Schooling seems to emphasise being *employable* and being ready to *earn* money. But *earning* money is a totally different skillset to managing or even creating money. For example, earning often involves:

- Developing skills and knowledge that can be performed for an employer or client in return for money.
- The ability to adapt and conform so that one is and remains attractive to an employer or client; and/or
- the ability to compete with others selling the same skillset.

But I know that someone who earns a high income can be totally inept with money and have none of the financial skills outlined above.

In schools we are groomed for earning money but not for financial success. At best we are taught a bit about managing finances and spending, but nothing about how to create wealth. Our kids are taught about using consumer credit wisely, but never about the skills needed to become rich. No wonder money causes so many problems for so many people! Any entrepreneurial advice at school is best summed up:

*"Build your own dreams or someone else
will hire you to build theirs!"*
Farrah Gray

We learn about money from the people around us

A cat's ability to hunt is completely defined by how good its mother was at hunting. In terms of the skills for financial success, we are a bit like cats: we learn from the key people around us. To be more specific we model other people's financial skills and often unconsciously. If you have money worries there is a high likelihood you have modelled someone's attitudes, skills and behaviours around money - often their prevailing mindset.

We differ from cats in one important aspect, however. We can choose to change. We can consciously upgrade our skills.

As I said in the Preface, growing up, I role modeled on financial struggle. We have all been influenced about money from those closest to us.

Whatever you have experienced in the past or currently experience around money will usually have its origins in a mindset modelled on someone influential - positive or adversely - in your past.

In any case, this book will show you - step-by-step - how to create a financially successful mindset.

Action Steps

Exploring Beliefs and Skills

1. Which currently feels *most* like you, right now?

- There's not enough money.
- Debt is bad.
- Don't waste money.
- Money comes from value-adding assets.

2. Starting with the obvious, consider what attitudes and beliefs about money you have absorbed from those around you, and how this might have impacted your financial success and whether your mindset needs to change.

Understand: you *do not* have to live your life according to the beliefs about money or of those around you. You can start to change your current money mindset at any time.

3. Understand that financial success is made up of the money skills – *creating, saving, managing, spending and giving money* – and that these can be learned by anyone at any time - including you.

Look for people who are successful with money who have any of these five skills. Ask them how they think about money and what they *do* to be so successful. You will be pleasantly surprised at how much you will learn.

Especially notice if you think something like, "I can't *do* that or *be* like them." That is your *current* limiting money mindset talking!

Chapter 2

What is a Mindset?

In this chapter I will outline the definition, structure and also the actual results caused by each of *The 4 Money Mindsets* and how each differs from the others. But first an entertaining tale.

The Tale of Two Travellers and the Farmer

A traveller came upon an old farmer hoeing in his field beside the road. Eager to rest his feet, the wanderer hailed the countryman, who seemed happy enough to straighten his back and talk for a moment.

"What sort of people live in the next town?" asked the stranger.

"What were the people like where you've come from?" replied the farmer, answering the question with another question.

"They were a bad lot. Troublemakers all and lazy too. The most selfish people in the world and not a one of them to be trusted. I'm happy to be leaving the scoundrels."

"Is that so?" replied the old farmer. "Well, I'm afraid that you'll find the same sort in the next town."

Disappointed, the traveller trudged on his way and the farmer returned to his work.

Some time later another stranger, coming from the same direction, hailed the farmer and they stopped to talk.

"What sort of people live in the next town?" he asked.

"What were the people like where you've come from?" replied the farmer once again.

"They were the best people in the world. Hard-working, honest and friendly. I'm sorry to be leaving them."

"Fear not," said the farmer. "You'll find the same sort in the next town."

What did you take from this story? I believe we create our own experiences in our minds and then consequently act from our own frame of reference when we come up against reality. And this can have a marked effect on the actual results we get from people and life.

Definition of Mindset

Before you read any further, what's your definition of mindset? What do you think it is and how does it work? How does it affect your life - positively or negatively? Can mindset influence or alter your behaviour?

A mindset is exactly what it suggests: how the mind is 'set' (often a bit like concrete) on any subject.

Mindset can been defined as a habitual mental attitude that determines how you will interpret, decide and ultimately respond to situations whether that mindset is appropriate and resourceful or not.

Mindsets can be positive or negative

Understand you were not born with a positive or a negative mindset. Mindset is learned. And therefore it can be changed at any time.

Psychologist Carol Dweck, performed extensive long-term research into mindset and identified two predominant mindsets - *fixed* and *growth*. Both are usually well established by the age of four. Either mindset shapes your view of the world, your potential, thinking and behaviours.

A *fixed* mindset limits and even inhibits thinking and behaviour. It blames circumstances for poor performance and tends to define the person. The overarching theme of a fixed mindset is: this is how things are and will always be and there is *no point trying* to change.

A *growth* mindset is cultivated by effort, entertains the possibility of change and improvement for the better and copes significantly better with challenges and setbacks regardless of circumstances which tend to *refine* that person. The overarching theme of a growth mindset is: if something isn't working for me, I can change it *if I try*.

Different mindsets, of course, do not guarantee success but they make the experience of life qualitatively better.

Importantly, Dweck discovered a *growth* mindset can be taught and changed at any stage of life.

This means if your current money mindset is not giving you the results you want you can learn a better mindset. You can change your beliefs. You are not locked in.

The question is: Do you want to change?

The Structure of Any Mindset

Mindsets have a structure. An easy way to understand the structure of a mindset is to think of it as being like an iceberg. The parts you can usually see comprise your *decisions, actions* and *results*. Actually that's the bit others often see more clearly than you!

But the parts you can see are not as important as feelings, thoughts, values and beliefs - the bits you can't see easily or at all. The following diagram will help:

The bits you can usually see/observe

Results

Actions

Decisions

*The underlying parts
of the mindset that drive results*

Thoughts

Feelings

Values

Beliefs

Your mindset is always composed of the underlying set of beliefs, values, feelings, thoughts and decisions; the bit you see is the actions and the results of those actions.

In summary:

Mindset =   Decisions, Actions Results
          Beliefs, Values, Feelings and Thoughts

For example, what you believe, value, think and feel about fashion determines your *fashion* mindset. So if you

* love clothes
* look up to fashion icons and designers and believe they are hugely important in your life

- put considerable time into thinking about and planning your clothes and appearance for every day and event like being with others who have a similar opinion
- are always dressed up to the nines
- feel good when your clothes are just right
- and make decisions to get the look you want

... you would have a *fashion* mindset.

Conversely, if you have an anti-fashion mindset where you ...

- believe 'the fashion establishment is wrong'
- are against labels, designers and brand names
- that 'people who spend a lot of time and money dedicated to fashion are frivolous, mindless 'followers'
- and make purchase decisions that support your beliefs
- think about where your clothes come from, and how and by whom they are produced
- feel anger at the exploitation caused by much of the fashion industry

... then your *anti-fashion* mindset will cause you to take actions that have different results from someone with a *fashion* mindset. Neither is better than the other; the two mindsets are just different.

How Mindsets Cause Results

Your beliefs, values, feelings, thoughts and decisions directly lead to your actions, and inevitably all of this will produce a predictable set of results. For example, the person with the fashion conscious mindset will look very different from the person with the anti-fashion mindset.

Every style or look in fashion that is a distinctive, unified manner of dress has its own mindset such as the 1980s *Sloane Ranger* look as do the Glamorous, Utilitarian, Power-dressing and Equestrian looks.

Any mindset will drive you to buy clothing, fabrics, brands, designers, styles in certain shops, and these actions inevitably lead to results. So others will see you as power-dressing, chic, sporty, punk, and so on. What they are seeing are the visible results of a deep mindset.

Therefore, your fashion mindset will directly drive the *decisions* you make and the *actions* you take regarding fashion. The clothes you are wearing right now, and those in your wardrobe, are a direct result of your fashion mindset. The mindset, in this case the way you do fashion, is the engine behind the results – the wardrobe you have and how you wear it right now.

Explore Your Mindsets

The point is you have mindsets about everything.

Your mindset about your boss, work, politics, health, diet, holidays, friends or whatever, is specific to you.

You might be aware of some of them, while many are so deep-set and habitual that you are hardly conscious they even exist. The best way to bring these into your awareness is to examine the physical results in your life. If you are thin and have always been thin, you have a *thin* mindset. If you have a tidy house and always have had a tidy house, then you have a *tidy* mindset.

Let's look at what a *tidy house* mindset might look like.

John believes a clean and tidy house is the sign of an organised mind and values having a tidy house very highly. John's thoughts and feelings will centre around how tidy his house is, so he will take certain actions to align his thoughts and feelings, which will result in a tidy house.

Mindset	Clean and tidy house
Beliefs/Values	Believe a clean and tidy house is a sign of an organised mind
Feelings	Feel calmer and more in control when the house is tidy. Feel stressed when the house is messy.
Thoughts	Tidy house is good; messy house is bad
Decisions	Prioritise time for tidying
Actions	Set aside time to tidy the house regularly. Tidy up.
Results	Very clean and tidy house. People admire how clean and tidy the house is.

Imagine someone has a mindset for being *slim*. Here is how their mindset might be organised.

Mindset	Slim
Beliefs/Values	Being slim Value the health benefits of being slim. Value dietary opinions of people who are slim.
Feelings	Don't like feeling fatter. Like feeling attractive.
Thoughts	People who are slim are in control. Eating correctly. Portion control. Not eating excessively. Low carb/low fat diet.
Decisions	Prioritise healthy food. I will eat less today if I ate more yesterday.

Actions	Choose healthy food. Eat the correct quantity to maintain a slim figure.
Results	Slim. Fairly consistent weight over time.

Imagine the *success* mindset of Victoria Beckham.

Mindset	Success
Beliefs/Values	I want to be a household name as well-known as *Persil Automatic*
Feelings	Feel good when successful Feel bad if I'm not recognised
Thoughts	How can I grow the brand? Focus on building my brand Unswerving focus on building my success
Decisions	Based on the right business and publicity Only do what makes me appear extremely successful
Actions	Business-focused Stand apart from former less successful colleagues
Results	Global profile Extremely successful fashion house Mediocre singer Entrepreneur Now even more successful than her famous and successful husband

Now imagine the *winning* mindset of a world class athlete.

Mindset	Winning
Beliefs/Values	I am Number One I am a winner You have to give everything to be the best
Feelings	Focus on the goal Pain but push through Joy on achievement Dogged determination
Thoughts	What do I need to do to get to Number One? Constantly figuring out what I need to do extra to be the best
Decisions	Train harder Take the best health decisions I will do what I need to do to give my best performance Set training goals
Actions	Sticks to training schedule Sticks to dietary requirements Hires an elite athlete coach
Results	Improving Winning Taking part

So far I've given you *positive* mindset examples. Now imagine the mindset of someone with a negative *procrastination* mindset.

Mindset	Procrastination
Beliefs/Values	It takes luck to achieve It is easier for others I'm/it's not (good) enough I need to know exactly what to do before I begin

Feelings	Feeling tired, bored, distracted
	Fear
	Self-doubt
	Lack of confidence
	Feeling guilty for time-wasting
Thoughts	Distracted
	It's not the right time
	This is hard
	It's not good enough
	I don't know what to do
Decisions	Doing low priority tasks first
	I'll just get an easier task done first
Actions	Only doing low priority tasks
	Putting things off
	Getting distracted
	Time-wasting / doing unproductive things
Results	Low achievement
	Time wasted
	Frustration at lack of achievement
	Envy/dislike of those who do achieve

What do you think the mindset of someone who is super healthy would be? Would it happen by accident or would it have something to do with what the individual does?

What do you think about someone who is in the top 25% in terms of income? Is that person's mindset random (besides those who have inherited or won money), or are they doing something different to others at a deeper level?

The goal is to reflect on what is happening in the areas of beliefs and values, feelings, thoughts, decisions, actions and results.

Action Steps

Finding the Mindsets
Behind the Results in Your Life

It is easier to look at the results you are getting in your life - the things you can observe and measure - and then work backwards.

You are getting results in many areas of your life. So take a few moments to look at some of the real results you are currently getting. List them in terms of health, wealth, relationships, etc. Next pick one area and trace *back* to actions, decisions, thoughts, feelings, values and beliefs. You might want to use the blank template on the next page.

Your Results and Mindset

Use the following table to look at the real results in your life. List your *results* in terms of health, wealth, relationships, etc, and trace them right *back* through results, actions, decisions, thoughts, feelings, to beliefs/values. You might also try *both* positive and negative results. For example, a mindset for being *overweight* or a *smoker*. For the best results, set aside enough uninterrupted time to do this exercise as designed. You can download a blank PDF A4 version of this template at:

www.4moneymindsets.com/resources.pdf

Did you do the exercise? If so, what have you learned?

Every real result in your life is the result of your mindsets. The good news is that mindsets can be changed if you don't like the results you are getting now.

	Results	Actions	Decisions	Thoughts	Feelings	Beliefs/Values
Health						
Wealth						
Happiness						
Relationships						

Chapter 3

What is a Money Mindset?

A money mindset specifically relates to money and produces real results. This means that your money mindset produces the financial results in your life.

I saw this principle in action very clearly when I worked as a debt adviser. My main driver for taking on this role was believing I might be able to help people in debt, because of my own childhood experiences.

"If I could just help people get out of debt, I thought, everything would be OK and their children would never have to go through what I did."

When I was six and my father's business was collapsing and we were losing everything all I wanted was for an adult to step in and take control and do what was needed to stop the debt getting worse. From my adult perspective, I can see now that meant putting a plan in place to restore positive cash flow.

However, as I went about my work as a debt adviser, I kept noticing that no matter how often I helped people, they would just go straight back into debt.

I finally realised that financial results are driven by a fixed money mindset when I worked with an elderly couple in 2009.

She was 76 and he was 75. When I visited their house, both were crying with anxiety and distress. Their bank had lent them £12,000, even though they were pensioners with no assets. Technically, at that point their home was no longer fully their own due to an equity release scheme.

I really felt for them, helped to resolve the situation and finally got the bank 'off their back'. Within a month I went on to work with their daughter, who was *also* in debt, as well as their son and a cousin. The whole family seemed to have the same type of spending patterns.

Soon their finances were under control.

Then six months later the father called me to say they were in debt again and could I please come and sort it out, *again*? I was lost for words!

At first I felt betrayed because I thought my work had really made a difference to the family. Then I felt angry. On reflection, I can see that those feelings of betrayal and anger said more about me than about them – these were about my own issues, as I had been reliving some of my childhood trauma while working with them.

Then the penny dropped. I realised this family had a fixed way of thinking about money. Being in-debt was the way they planned their finances. They would always get into debt no matter how much money they might have. Being in-debt was their mindset.

Unless they changed their beliefs, values, thoughts, feelings and decisions about money, they would remain in-debt. And the results would be both predictable and inevitable throughout their lives.

Introducing the 4 Money Mindsets

Over time I began to see this same *In-debt* mindset again and again.

Once I understood how the mindset of my debt advice clients worked, I began to research further. Comparing them with people who were not in-debt, it became clear that there were a number of distinct money mindsets, each producing different results.

By analysing the key beliefs and values, feelings and thoughts about financial success in relation to the actual finances of these people, I was able to identify four specific money mindsets: *rich, comfortable, break-even* and *in-debt*.

Rich

This group believes they are 'entirely responsible for their financial success'.

In their view financial success is available to anyone, although some might have had a much better starting point than others.

Financial success is the result of hard work and drive, the ability to leverage any available resources, delayed gratification, risk-taking, overcoming obstacles and dogged persistence.

Importantly, they create wealth and use their assets and ability to leverage and add value.

Comfortable

People in this group believe they 'must work to be financially secure'.

In their view, financially secure people make sure they save for a rainy day. They believe everyone should strive to make themselves financially secure, and that security is the result of consistently saving money and never ever spending more than you earn. Delayed gratification is their maxim. They feel resentful of people who get into debt and then expect a bailout.

Their money comes by way of exchanging or 'selling' their time and skills and they feel that the only way to accumulate money, is to work much harder or have a stroke of luck (like a lottery win!). If they need more money for something unexpected they will, very reluctantly, dip into savings.

Break-even

People in this category believe that 'getting into debt is bad', and that people should learn to manage on what they have.

In their view financial success equates to always paying bills on time and never getting into debt. They often feel that 'people like them' could never be very rich, and that they have little control over the amount of money they can bring into their lives; so they simply have to make do with what they've got.

Money comes from exchanging their time and skills, or from pension or welfare and like the *Comfortable* group they believe the only way to get more of it is to work much harder or through a stroke of luck.

Saving extra cash is impossible because there is always something that has to be paid for.

Any unexpected expenses will have to come from living expenses, which means they will go without until the next payment comes in. If that isn't possible, they will further defer payment and do without something else. They will avoid going into debt if they can, but if the expense is large enough to warrant it, they will pay it down as quickly as possible – to get back to break-even point.

In-debt

These people believe that they just 'do not have enough money no matter what they do'. They feel that as soon as they get money, a portion will go to pay off debts then the rest will be gone soon after.

This group often spends on others through feelings of guilt or duty, and finds it difficult to delay gratification. If they unexpectedly need extra money, they will borrow it.

'Delayed gratification' and 'impulse control' are two primary skills of human behaviour. Someone with a diminished ability to delay gratification will invariably have money worries. They are typically at the mercy of impulsive shopping sprees.

Your financial records tell the story

You can see these mindsets very clearly from the financial records of an individual, couple, family or business.

Even if someone with an in-debt mindset wins the lottery, within a few years much, if not all, of the money will be gone. We have all heard stories of people coming into vast fortunes and blowing the lot!

I remember the story of Evelyn Adams, from New Jersey, who won the state lottery twice! Within a short time she lost her $5.4 million total winnings and ended up living in a trailer. "Winning the lottery isn't always what it's cracked up to be," she said.

Peter had a fabulous job in London and earned a significant salary. By the time he was in his 30s, his widowed mother had helped him buy a tiny apartment and bailed him out of debt several times. He avoided bankruptcy twice. He inherited a sizeable fortune and spent the lot within two years. He then re-mortgaged his flat to fund his lifestyle as property prices rose in London.

The more money he had access to, the more he spent. A couple of big pay rises at work allowed him to borrow more and more. Eventually his debts exceeded his mother's assets so she was unable to help him any more. Bankruptcy was inevitable.

Our work together led to him rebuilding his relationship with money and changing his mindset, so that he never ends up bankrupt again.

Each mindset is driven by its own distinct sequence of money flow, which we will examine in the next chapter.

Action Steps

- You know yourself pretty well. So which mindset sounds the most like you, right now? Why do you think that?
- Write a brief money biography that shows the patterns of your thinking and behaviour about money.

Part 2

Money Skills

Chapter 4

Skills for Keeping and Growing Money

In Chapter 1, I introduced five financial success skills - *giving, spending, managing, saving* and *creating*. In this chapter we explore them further from both a positive and negative perspective As you read this chapter notice any traits that sound like you.

Giving money

We all give money, be it to friends, family, charities or the people we interact with on a day to day basis. The skill of giving correctly and our choices around giving money or choosing not to give are critical to our overall financial success.

Knowing when to give, to whom, for what and how much is the key.

Positive Giving Skills

Giving the right amount

Not giving makes us smaller. Giving allows us to use the fabulous power of money to do good, either to treat someone or make a difference in their life.

It is critical that you give an amount that will help the receiver, but do not give so much that you end up with financial problems of your own.

Giving money should never mean taking someone else's problem and making it yours. For example, if your adult child has a debt they can't repay and you take it on, leaving you with a debt you can't repay, you have damaged yourself financially – and not helped them to develop the financial skills they need for success. As best selling author Andrew Priestley says in his book *The Money Chimp*, "Giving should not hurt the giver."

Giving at the right time

It is important to give when someone needs help. If someone's life could be changed for the better by your financial help, then it is definitely the right time to give.

A friend of mine knew a single parent who had been involved in a terrible accident. My friend paid for specialist physiotherapy that made a huge difference to the quality of the woman's life, and her children.

It is also important that you don't give at a time when it harms your own finances. For example, if you really want to give to someone but lack the funds then wait until you do have enough money.

Giving to the right cause or person

The recipient should be something or someone you believe in. You should not give because you feel pressured or made to feel guilty.

Giving for the right reason

Give as much as you can and give often because giving is good for everyone involved. Give because it feels right for you and because you believe the recipient would really benefit, not to have power over or induce obligation or guilt.

Giving without expecting anything in return

It's a good exercise occasionally to give to someone who doesn't know you who you will never meet again.

It is really nice to treat people, and good to be able to share the fruits of your financial success. Giving while expecting something in return leads to resentment, damaged relationships, or even loss of deep friendships.

Key Negative Markers
- or Lack of Giving Skills

Abdicating

This refers to handing over money when you know the other person should take financial responsibility for themselves.

One man had an alcoholic daughter who claimed she could not work because she kept getting fired. He supported her financially throughout her life, even buying her a house. Of course she stayed a non-working alcoholic all her life. Had he withdrawn financial support when she was a young adult, there is a chance she might have realised that the only possibility of success would be for her to take responsibility for herself.

It takes courage and conviction to say no to someone whose financial skills are undeveloped, especially if you are close. A brave and caring person understands that everyone needs to learn financial skills and responsibility, and not expect someone else to be accountable for them.

Keeping all your money and never giving any

Never giving is a sorry state of affairs. A client of mine had over £80,000 in a savings account and a high salary of around £5,000 a month. When we worked together, we discovered that he always felt poor and short of money. He never gave money to anyone because he felt he never had enough to spare.

I set him an exercise to give without any expectation of return. We agreed that he would set an amount that would be a stretch for him, but still doable. After a month he came back and revealed that he had given £5 to a charity. I felt sad for him because he was just as mean to himself as he was to everyone else.

Giving when you should not be giving

Lending money

If someone asks you if they can *borrow* money from you, beware! If you would not have given it as a gift without being asked – then don't do it. More often than not you will not get it back. This is why a great many relationships are soured if not ruined. Either give as a gift or say no.

Working for clients with a record of non-payment

This affects some people's financial success enormously, because they do not pursue those who owe them money; some even continue to work for people who repeatedly pay very late or often not at all. I know a fabulous builder who is owed tens of thousands of pounds by non-paying clients … many of whom he has returned to work for again.

Undercharging

Undercharging for your services is technically giving away your wealth. Understand, if you undercharge you might find it difficult to achieve financial success.

Spending Money

Some people believe 'there is no skill in spending money, anyone can do it!' To others, spending on anything that is not absolutely necessary should be avoided and the very cheapest option is what they choose every time.

However, as my research progressed it became apparent that many people identified 'spending money wisely' as a critical component of financial success. This is what personal finance advisor and best selling author, Ramit Sethi would call 'conscious spending'.

Positive Spending Skills

Understanding that money is a tool to be used wisely to make your life better

The ability to see the financial 'Big Picture'

Your spending decisions should ideally be in line with your overall financial goals. For you, this might be financial freedom at 50, travelling the world at 40, or retiring and opening a donkey sanctuary at 60.

Whatever your long-term aim is you must have a financial plan to achieve it. If you have allocated a great deal of your existing money for savings and investments or building a business, an impulsive purchase not critical to your goal could easily set you back or completely derail your future life plans.

- Making spending decisions in line with your overall financial strategy.
- Buying with your long-term goals in mind.
- Spending as much as you can afford on the things that really matter to you is what creates your desired lifestyle.

Being so frugal that you sacrifice things that matter to you is not spending money wisely. Not using money that you have can make your life hard, uncomfortable or downright miserable. The key here is to spend as much as you can (without derailing your long term financial goals) on what you value, rather than spending on unimportant things you don't value. For example, we spend on education (extra tuition and school fees) because we value it, but don't spend extra on cars because that's not important to us.

Key Negative Indicators – Spending Mistakes

- Not understanding that money is a tool to be used wisely to make your life better.
- Making spending decisions that make your life worse in the longer term, for example, buying cheap unhealthy food when you can afford good quality food will cause health issues in the long run.
- Not spending on things that really matter to you. If going out, or cars, or an obscure hobby is really important to you, then use some of your money for that.
- Spending when you cannot afford to.
- Spending on credit cards or finance plans to buy anything that is not of high priority.
- Impulse buying, instead of delaying gratification
- Short term gain, long term pain.

- Not seeking the best price.
- Buying purely for price and not value.
- Keeping up with the Jones's.
- Falling for marketing/selling hype.
- Not thoroughly understanding any finance deal/product you are taking on.
- Getting pressured into spending.

Spending Money You Don't Have

Choosing to spend borrowed money is spending money you don't have. Unless you keep it firmly under control and to a minimum, this habit will severely impede your financial success.

Paying Bills or Money You Owe, Late

This is about the importance of making payments or giving back money owed on time, a subject not often talked about.

Sometimes we pay late, believing that finding money for the payment will be too hard and that those we owe won't miss it or be aversely affected. Some even feel 'entitled' to pay late, and declare that the other party should have budgeted for a late payment. One parent I know had a child who attended a small, struggling private school. The fees, which went directly to pay the teachers, had to be paid at the beginning of each term but they chose to pay at the end of the year – and felt entitled to do so. It caused cash flow issues for the school but the staff did not want to ask him to take their child out of the school for the child's sake.

Occasionally people have to be chased to hand over money they owe. This can lead to big financial problems, as the offender becomes known for being a late payer and gets a bad credit rating.

Not Repaying

In 2008, working as a debt adviser, I saw how some people ended up in a toxic spiral of debt through a catastrophic life event such as an accident, health crisis, job loss or divorce. Some situations were heart-breaking, but I was amazed and inspired by the ones who afterwards got themselves and their finances back on track, turning their lives round. Often this would take years of hard work and determination.

However, I also saw many with a chronic pattern of borrowing and not repaying. Some of these people were well off yet still had poor ethics and skills in this area.

Not repaying the money agreed for a service, product or loan already consumed, is a deliberate choice some people make. They often believe they will repay the debt 'someday', or else just ignore the repayment requests, reasoning that the person or business that trusted them to pay doesn't need the money as much as they do.

I have seen many cases where the borrower feels entitled to the money and resentful at any attempts to recover it, firmly believing that they are being victimised by the person who wants – and has a right – to be paid.

When working as a debt adviser I often saw people turn first to friends and family when borrowing money. Failing or refusing to give back what they had promised frequently led to families falling out, lost and broken friendships, bitterness, resentment and broken trust. In some cases, the family member or friend had lent money they couldn't afford to lose and ended up financially compromised.

The recalcitrant borrowers, having exhausted all the softer options, would then borrow from institutions and loan sharks – who knew their patterns and would intimidate them to redeem the money.

Managing Money

I was taught the skill of managing money at school in Ireland, 35 years ago.

The subject was called *Home Economics*, though it was nothing like the 'Food Technology' education our kids now get. The focus was on keeping a good home and table, making sure everyone had what they needed (food, basic clothing, etc) and top marks were given for making a little go a long way. We were taught how to make cheap nutritious meals, learning what constituted true value in terms of food and what was just more expensive because of a perception of being better when in fact it wasn't.

We discovered that cheap and expensive cuts of meat have the same nutritional content and with expensive branded goods, most of the cost was paying for that branding.

We learned how to turn any leftovers into a meal, how to make clothes last longer and how to repair them, how to minimise fuel consumption costs, how to decorate, make bed linen, clothing and a myriad other household management techniques.

My granny and auntie were brilliant at managing money. Auntie Eva used to boil a kettle of water in the morning and store it in a thermos for tea throughout the day rather than repeatedly using the fuel for reboiling it.

To manage money, they used the 'Three Jars' method: one jar for rent and bills, one jar for upcoming expenses such as school uniforms and shoes and so on, and the last jar for family consumption such as food and treats.

There was one very important rule. Once the jar was empty that was it. No more spending until money came in again and the jar was replenished. Doing without was common.

Positive Money Management Skills

- Prioritising spending.
- Allocating money for specific purposes.
- Cleverly stretching resources and food, up-cycling clothing etc, to make a little money go a long way.
- Planning the use of resources to ensure everyone has what they need (not always what they want).
- Always having enough resources to do what you need.

Key Negative Indicators
– or Lack of Money Management Skills

- Not prioritising spending decisions properly.
- Wasting food, energy or money on unnecessary items.
- Spending too much and not being able to cover a bill.
- Not having enough resources as a result of being wasteful.
- Not planning for upcoming expenses.
- Not keeping track of spending.
- Not adjusting spending decisions in line with priorities and how much is left.

Saving Money

The key skill for saving money is to pay yourself first. Save a specified amount every payday before you spend anything. Automate this, so it's easy and never becomes an issue. People who are good at saving invariably amass large sums. They will have set aside the 'emergency fund' and six months' living expenses that all financially successful people allow for. They will also have savings for investment goals and the future.

Positive Saving Skills

- Paying yourself first. Always, no matter what.
- Being good at spotting financial risk.
- Getting the best rates on financial deals on savings accounts, financial products and pensions.
- Automating accounts to ensure you save money.
- Not spending your savings.
- Having savings goals.

Key Negative Indicators – or Lack of Saving Skills

- Spending your savings.
- Not saving first or automating your savings.
- Not deferring gratification.
- Being a care free spendthrift.
- Not having any savings.

Creating Money

There are two keys to creating money: *value* and *leverage*. Those who are skilled at creating money save to invest.

Creating Value

Creating value is all about creating goods or services that another person or group values enough to exchange money for. Examples include items of food, clothing, online training courses, apps, distribution channels – in fact, anything that somebody else is willing to pay for. The essence in the creation is to produce something that makes or sells for more money than it cost to put the constituent parts together. This is the first step to wealth creation.

Creating Leverage

Leverage is the ability to use resources to speed up wealth creation. We are all equal in having 24 hours in a day. The difference comes from how we use it! Somebody who earns £10 an hour and saves will take a long time to reach the sum of £1,000,000. Very few people earn enough to save that amount even over many years. A person who understands the power of leverage can reach this amount much faster.

The more a person learns to use leverage, the faster his or her financial growth.

People who successfully employ leverage accomplish exponentially more in the same time than those who don't!

Types of Leverage

There are four critical types of leverage that enable you to achieve maximum success in the shortest possible time.

- Other people's money.
- Other people's time.
- Other people's knowledge.
- Technology.

Let's look at each in turn.

Other People's Money

Financial leverage is using money belonging to others to significantly increase the yields you can achieve on the assets you invest in.

For example, if you invest £1,000 and receive an annual return of £100, you have realised a yield of 10%, and your £1,000 has grown to £1,100.

Example 1	Investment, No Leverage
Start amount	£1,000
Invest for 1 year	10%
Increase	£100
End amount	£1,100
Yield on investment	10%

If you used the same £1,000, but borrowed an additional £9,000, and invested £10,000 with the same yield percentage of 10%, you would have made a return of £1,000, or 10 times as much as under the original scenario. If the cost of borrowing the money is £500 over the borrowing period, you will still realise a net return of £500 on your original £1,000 (£1,000 being the entire sum that you personally brought to the table at the outset). This is a 50% yield, which is significantly higher than realised by the investment of your original £1,000 alone.

Example 2	Investment, With Leverage
Start amount	£1,000
Borrow	£9,000
Total to Invest	£10,000
Invest for 1 year	10%
Increase	£1000
Cost of Borrowing	£500
End amount	£1,500
Yield on investment	50%

Using £9,000 in borrowed money and only £1,000 of your own money is a typical example of financial leverage as used in property investing.

Some professional investors are able to reduce their investment contribution in a given opportunity to substantially less than 10% of the total amount invested, thus further boosting yields.

Using Margin to Buy Stock

Another example of financial leverage is the use of margin to buy stocks. Margin is essentially a loan, where a brokerage firm lends money to an investor to buy more stock. This comes at a cost and carries risk.

Interest is paid on this loan, and if the value of the stocks pledged as collateral decreases below a preset limit, the investor will experience a 'margin' call, where he or she will have to deposit further cash or securities to cover possible losses.

The purchase of stocks on margin is a tool used by many rich people. For example, a share in Fred & Co costs £5. An ordinary investor has £1,000 to invest and buys two hundred shares. The shares increase in price by 25% so the investor makes £250.

Example 3	Buying Shares, No Leverage
Share price	£5 each per share
Invest	£1,000 in buying 200 shares
Share price increase	25%
Increase	£250
End amount	£1,250
Profit	£250

Using leverage, an investor borrows £10,000 on margin at 15% interest (£1,500). The shares increase by 25% so he makes £2,500. He repays £1,500 making £1,000.

Example 4	Buying Shares, Using Margin as Leverage
Share price	£5 each per share
Invest	£10,000 in buying 2,000 shares
Share price increase	25%
Increase	£2,500
Cost of Borrowing	£1,500
End amount	£11,000
Profit	£1,000
	(£2,500 increase - £1,500 borrowing cost

Options

An option is where you have the right but not the obligation to buy something for a given price in the future.

For an investor, being able to buy an option provides inherent financial leverage. You do not need to borrow capital to buy options, which means that you can control a larger number of shares with your initial investment amount than if you purchased the shares themselves.

For example, if you had £1,000 you could purchase 10 shares of Fred & Co stock valued at £100 per share. Or you could buy option contracts that might be valued at £200 for lots of 100 shares (£2 per option). For your investment of £1,000, you could buy five options contracts, increasing your financial leverage by allowing you to control 500 shares instead of just 10. First consider the case of just buying shares directly.

Example 5	Buying Shares, No Leverage
Amount to invest	£1,000
Share price	£100 each
Invest	£1,000 in buying 10 shares
Share price increase	25%
Profit	£250

If, during the option contract, the value of those shares rises substantially, you could buy the shares that you have the right to buy at the agreed price (strike price), which at that point is much lower than the market value. You can then resell those shares at market value, generating a profit on a much larger number of shares than the ones you would have purchased originally if you had bought the 10 shares with your £1,000.

To execute this trade, you would need to have access to a lot more capital in order to purchase the shares that your options entitle you to buy (albeit for a short time only) and be willing to take the risk of the market price suddenly dropping before you have the opportunity to resell your shares. Let's say the strike price of the shares is £100 and the value of the shares increases by 25% as before. You agree to exercise your option to buy the shares once they reach this value of increase.

Example 6	Buying Shares using Options as Leverage
Amount to invest	£1,000
Buy 500 Share Options	£2 each
Shares reach 25%	(Pre-arranged strike rate)
Exercise your option to buy 500 shares for £100 per share (pre-arranged strike rate)	£50,000
Share value	£62,500
Take away your cost of shares and options	(£50,000)
	(£1,000)
	£51,000
Profit	£11,500

The best source of financial leverage in this investment comes from the fact that the percentage increase on the option is proportionately higher than the increase of the underlying share. This leverage also comes without the risk of investing the much greater amounts of capital needed to buy and sell the shares the options give you the right to buy instead.

In the hypothetical purchase mentioned previously, let's say that the value of the shares increases from £100 per share to £125 per share.

If you bought those 10 shares, the profit on your investment of £1,000 would be £250, or a 25% increase.

On the other hand, spending £1,000 to generate £11,500 is an increase of over 1,000%. This much higher potential increase is how trading options can effectively create leverage. Of course the potential loss is also higher, but your exposure is limited to £1000. Understanding financial leverage, the advantages and risks, is very important in trading options. With good trading strategies, using leverage can allow you to maximise your returns, while minimising the risk.

Expansion

Other examples of financial leverage include companies borrowing money to expand operations. The benefit of the leverage comes from increased property value or higher company revenue, which raises the value of stockholders' shares. Rich people learn to use financial leverage. They start small, continually learning and leveraging, until they have larger amounts to leverage.

Other People's Time

The use of financial leverage alone is not sufficient to accelerate financial growth to the maximum. To build wealth more quickly, leveraging other people's time is vital. Those with a rich money mindset strategically plan how to leverage others' time in their personal and business lives.

The majority of the population fail to grasp the importance of implementing multiple leverage strategies, so when they think of making more money they think in terms of working more hours. This type of linear thinking is contrary to the way most rich individuals view the world.

Leveraging Time

Let's look at a specific example. Assume you have set up a contract to manufacture garments. You are manufacturing 10,000 a week at 10p each. That gives you £1,000 a week.

You either need to clone yourself or leverage more time to achieve success. If you employ 20 employees at £300 each per week, and each of them produces 10,000 garments a week, that will give you 200,000 garments a week, giving you £20,000 a week.

Take away £6,000 for wages and £4,000 for other expenses associated with a bigger operation, and you are now making £10,000 a week.

You have effectively leveraged your time through others resulting in a 10-fold increase in your profits for inputting the same amount of time.

Examples of the use of time leverage are almost infinite, ranging from building a business with contract or salaried employees to hiring a decorator to paint your house while you improve your leverage systems. If you intend to achieve significant wealth, you must not only focus on the use of financial leverage, but also on finding creative ways to leverage the time of others in a win-win fashion, resulting in positive financial returns.

Other People's Knowledge

In addition to time and financial leverage, it is also essential to leverage the knowledge and skills of others. This is not only through studying others' knowledge through books, recordings, seminars, blogs and forums, but also through using others' talents to achieve greater output than you can generate alone.

I have seen business people waste months learning to build a mediocre website rather than pay someone to build a great one giving them time to focus on growing their business. Rich people build a team of people that have the knowledge that their business needs in order to grow.

There is a story about Henry Ford, an entrepreneur who really understood how to develop significant wealth.

During an interview, a reporter was trying to show that Henry was not very intelligent by continually asking technical questions.

When Ford could not answer, the reporter started to berate him about his lack of knowledge but Ford simply responded by picking up the phone and putting the question to one of his employees. After another question he did the very same thing. Then he turned to the reporter and said, "I don't need to know all of the answers to run a successful company. I have hired people to answer these questions for me so I can concentrate on steering the ship."

To achieve maximum wealth and success, surround yourself with people whose knowledge you can leverage for greater growth.

Technology

Finally, to achieve financial success in this digital age, it is essential to leverage technology, particularly the internet. The digital age is an exciting revolution and we are living through it right now. Associated technologies allow operational efficiency and a level of sophistication that cannot be otherwise achieved.

We have all heard of young billionaires who achieve incredible wealth by leveraging technology before the age of 25.

The large corporation with huge investments in resources ranging from property, staff, IT systems and money is now just one way of doing business – albeit a more traditional one. Taking the more agile example of e-commerce, anyone might be capable of sourcing or creating a product, selling globally, collecting payments and dispatching goods with ease, using current technology and, of course, all from their own home.

It infinitely increases our ability to connect with others, particularly through social media, which enables the creation of niche markets and the formation of a *Tribe*: a group of individuals who love and believe in what you offer, and will happily promote your product or service. Forming and building a brand is now within the reach of every new business owner.

The ability to systemise and automate processes (data management, customer contact, outsourcing) frees time and resources that allow sustainable growth and wealth generation. In business, connection is vital to growth and survival and without successfully leveraging technology, any business will be limited.

Action Steps

Go back through the five financial skills and the positive and negative traits for *giving, spending, managing, saving* and *creating*.

Which ones are most like you? Can you think of specific examples that relate to you personally and professionally?

Especially reread the section to do with *Creating, value* and *leverage*. Did you actually stop and think about the value/leverage case studies? Or did you skip over them?

If you have anything other than a *Rich* mindset this section will feel unfamiliar and you probably felt it didn't apply to you and simply skim-read that section.

So stretch yourself and reread the *Creating* section.

Part 3

The 4 Money Mindsets

Chapter 5

The 4 Money Mindsets

As we have seen in Chapter 3, a money mindset is a fixed attitude specifically relating to money. And *your* money mindset is the cause of *your* current financial state.

My research led me to discover four distinct money mindsets: *Rich, Comfortable, Break-Even* and *In-Debt*. In each individual, one of these will be dominant and thus dictate their financial situation.

Money Mindset 1 – Rich

Those who run a *Rich* money mindset habitually focus on adding value and leveraging resources. They see resources all around them, such as time, money, skills or technology, and are driven to leverage them.

What does 'leveraging resources' mean? The definition from the Business Dictionary is: "The ability to influence a system or an environment, that multiplies the outcomes of one's efforts without a corresponding increase in the consumption of resources."

In simple terms, leveraging is devising a way to use a resource so that the input is much less than the output, that is, doing a lot with a little or creating a big output with a significantly smaller input. People with a *Rich* money mindset understand this is the only way of making yourself rich.

When I asked rich people what someone who is savvy with money would do with fresh funds, they invariably said, "Leverage it". Very few people understand the concept of leverage and, as a result, continue to work harder than ever to make ends meet, wondering, "How come the rich get all the luck and we never seem to get ahead?"

The Rich Use Leverage

Creating money is a skill that people with a *Rich* money mindset have mastered.

An individual with a *Rich* money mindset uses the resources they have, such as time, money, other people, technology, and all sorts of other things, as tools to create money. Rich people don't trade time for money; rather, they use their time to add value and leverage resources.

The rich person always uses money with a purpose. He sees money as a tool that can be used to meet his needs, using it firstly to generate more money, and secondly to improve his quality of life – in that order.

Only when the leveraged resources are throwing off enough money does he buy the trappings of wealth such as cars, holidays and property. The rich are always thinking about how money can be made to work.

In response to my 7 Key Questions ...

- What is money?
- How do you get your money?
- What do you do with it once you get it?
- If you need more money, how do you get it?
- What would someone who is good with money do with it, once they get it?
- How do rich people get rich?
- How do poor people become poor?

... a clear *sequence* of actions specific to the *Rich* money mindset emerges:

- Leverage
- Give
- Spend

In other words, someone with a *Rich* mindset leverages money first, gives next, then spends what is generated by leveraging. When they save money, it is to leverage in the future.

Examples of the Rich Money Mindset

My great grandfather

My great grandfather William Roche founded Roches Stores, a chain of department stores, investing his time, money and all the funds he could save and borrow into building his business. The story goes he slept under the escalator on a straw mattress that was so uncomfortable he could be sure of rising every morning at 5am.

He did not marry until he was 40 because he knew he would not be able to give his family the time they deserved until he had successfully built his business.

He did enjoy the luxuries and trappings of wealth, but only once the business could sustain continuous investment and provide surplus money.

Leverage

First, he leveraged everything he could: money, time and other people's skills. This took a long time.

Spend

After he had built and grown the business only then did he spend money on the trappings of wealth.

My uncle

One of my relatives was also an individual with a rich money mindset. He created wealth by building a very successful storage business, eventually sold the business and retired. After achieving that, he spent time on his boat and hobbies – in other words, spending his money and his time.

Later on, he came into an unexpected and significant sum of money. However, instead of spending it on luxuries, he immediately used the funds to start and build another business!

He borrowed more money and hired staff to create more wealth. This was probably his sixth or seventh business – he was driven by this mindset.

The Structure of the Rich Money Mindset

Below are 12 working examples of the *Rich* Money Mindset. Read each one carefully to see what resonates with you and what doesn't. Note the ones that inspire you.

Example 1

Beliefs	I am 100% responsible for my financial success
Values	It is important to understand how to succeed financially I must learn how to leverage every opportunity around me
Feelings	Accept feeling challenged by being out of comfort zone Satisfaction at every financial success Feel responsible for how much money I have in my life I feel uneasy if something is wasting my time or money
Thoughts	What do I need to do to succeed financially? I focus on anything to do with financial success Finding opportunities to get out of my comfort zone is critical to getting rich
Decisions	Only do things that help me or move me towards financial success Don't complain
Actions	Only spend time and money where financial success will be generated
Results	Financial success

Example 2

Beliefs	You must create value to get rich
Values	It is important to know how to create value
Feelings	Happiness when I am adding value; frustration when I am not
Thoughts	What problems do people have? What do they want? Where can I add value?
Decisions	Focus only on activities that add value
Actions	Try new things to see if people want/value it enough to give money in exchange
Results	Products or services that people are willing to pay for

Example 3

Beliefs	You must leverage to get rich
Values	It is important to know how to leverage resources
Feelings	Happiness/exhilaration when leveraging is effective Frustration when leveraging is not working
Thoughts	Continually considering possible business models for every resource I can control
Decisions	Ensure all resources are maximising their return Any that are not must be changed and made to generate wealth
Actions	Take calculated risks with resources to generate maximum wealth
Results	Money-producing assets Control of resources that produce money Multiple income streams

Example 4

Beliefs	Time is worth more than money Working smarter not harder is the only way to get rich
Values	It is vital that I only focus my time on things that will produce the results I want in my life Focus on building wealth
Feelings	I can *feel* when I'm focussing on the wrong thing
Thoughts	Focus and prioritise the thoughts that will deliver my goal I understand exactly which activities advance me towards my goal and those that take me further away
Decisions	Choose only to do things that advance me towards my goals
Actions	Only do the right activities that lead to achieving the goal Spend time with others who are building wealth
Results	Achieves wealth goals

Example 5

Beliefs	You must take action to create wealth
Values	Making things happen is critical The importance of action in getting rich cannot be underestimated
Feelings	Happy when achieving; dissatisfied / frustrated when actions do not produce positive results Out of comfort zone – actions lead to getting to the next level
Thoughts	What action can I take to move this forward? I understand the difference between action and activity
Decisions	Decide on the best actions to take Prioritise only wealth-growing actions

Actions	Take calculated risks Take the right actions Never sell time in exchange for money Avoid activities that will not lead to wealth creation
Results	Wealth Does not sell time for money Cumulative action produces wealth-producing assets Has more skills than previously

Example 6

Beliefs	You must continually change and learn to become rich You have to learn how to become rich
Values	It is important to get better and take things to the next level if you want to be rich
Feelings	Enjoyment of change and a challenge Enjoy the struggle to get to the next level
Thoughts	Learning and change are necessary for getting rich
Decisions	Seek out learning opportunities Relentlessly seek out new people and ideas
Actions	Instigate change Take calculated risks Learn new things to apply to businesses
Results	Change Able to do things that was not able to do before Knows lots of different people

Example 7

Beliefs	Wealth creation begins with me, in my head. I have to figure it out
Values	It is important to figure out how to create wealth-generating systems It is important to know how to get rich
Feelings	Insatiable curiosity about how other successful people do things Driven to develop wealth-creation systems
Thoughts	I want control Considers systems and strategies for wealth creation Solves problems that others can't and turns the solution into a system
Decisions	Seek out people and resources to trail and create systems
Actions	Build teams and control resources
Results	Assets Businesses Investments

Example 8

I deserve to be rich	I deserve to be rich (I actually deserve to be rich)
Values	I am important and what I want out of life is important
Feelings	Clear about what I want
Thoughts	I know what I want and will ask for it I want wealth I set wealth-building goals
Decisions	Make decisions based on what I want and what I consider to be important
Actions	Only do things that meet my needs and lead to achieving what I want
Results	Desired level of wealth Systems that generate wealth and cash flow

Example 9

Beliefs	I believe in myself
Values	My self-belief is critical. It is the most important thing in getting what I want
Feelings	Overcomes any self-doubt Driven by self-belief
Thoughts	I am successful, and will succeed at anything I give sufficient focus to I will make it happen
Decisions	Never give up A setback is something to be overcome Never listen to self-doubting little voices in my head Don't let detractors dent self-belief
Actions	Keep going Do a bit every day Keep believing in myself and what I'm doing
Results	Achieves the desired results

Example 10

Beliefs	I set my own course in life
Values	Having control, power and freedom to choose my life is vital
Feelings	I love having freedom Excitement I feel in charge of my own life
Thoughts	I'm not taking orders from someone else I do not define myself by the limitations other people define themselves by I'm not one of the crowd
Decisions	Not dissuaded by negative feedback Don't be put off by others dragging you back
Actions	Make my own decisions
Results	Has the life they want Lives life differently to the average person Doesn't work for money

Example 11

Beliefs	Money is a tool
Values	The better I learn to use and get the tool, the richer my life will be
Feelings	I feel good and confident in my ability to stretch myself to create the money I need
Thoughts	Contemplate what I need to do to have all the money I need
Decisions	Decide upon actions that will create money and use it to make my life better
Actions	Use money skilfully
Results	Lives a rich life

Example 12

Beliefs	You must continually change and learn to become rich.
Values	It is important to get better and take things to the next level if you want to be rich.
Feelings	Enjoyment of change and a challenge Enjoy the struggle to get to the next level
Thoughts	Learning and change are necessary for getting rich.
Decisions	Seek out learning opportunities Relentlessly seek out new people and ideas
Actions	Instigate change Take calculated risks Learn new things to apply to business
Results	Change Able to do things that was not able to do before Knows lots of different people

It is worth reviewing this section again carefully because this is based on a good cross-section of wealthy client case studies - people who consistently leverage money. In some cases they have rebuilt their wealth from scratch. Now you can see exactly how they think about money!

Money Mindset 2 – Comfortable

Those who habitually run a *Comfortable* money mindset are driven *to* save. When they get any money they initially save a proportion and live on the rest. These people often have large savings and could survive for a considerable length of time if their source of income dried up.

If they invest, it is to save, for example, through shares or a modest portfolio of property to prop up their pension. Savings include retirement funds, institutional investment schemes or any types of savings or investment schemes run by someone else and sold by a broker, as well as cash.

People with a *Comfortable* money mindset save for the future or a rainy day rather than to buy something specific.

The most noticeable thing about those with this mindset is that they can tolerate quite a bit of discomfort. They are masters at delayed gratification.

The need to save is a huge driver. They see financial threats everywhere and save to create a buffer between them and the harsh financial world outside.

Responses to the Key Questions consistently reveal the sequence of actions specific to the *Comfortable* money mindset.

- Save
- Give
- Spend

Essentially, someone with a *Comfortable* money mindset will save, then give, and only spend what is necessary.

It is notable than when someone with this mindset invests, they do so *not to lose*, rather than invest more and work at it to guarantee success. They often say things like: *"don't invest anything you can't afford to lose."*

They also have no system or exit strategy or plan for what to do with the profit, instead just keeping it for a rainy day. Sadly this attitude often causes them to lose money, as they don't know what to do if things don't go according to plan. They tend to either panic and sell with the heard, or hang on in there hoping things will come right when they won't. The only chance of success in these circumstances is to make a rich money mindset decision and because they don't know how to, they just focus on minimising loss.

This sequence of financial actions is also clear from the individual's financial records. You can see the flow of money very clearly from their bank statements:

- Save
- Give
- Spend

Examples of the Comfortable Money Mindset

I have spoken with many individuals with a *Comfortable* money mindset. They are all motivated by a fear of financial insecurity. Their strategy is to save their income, clear down debt and live on little.

My father

I remember my father describing his job as a living hell and he likened waiting for retirement as a prison sentence. When he came into a significant sum of money he kept working and invested in shares. He did not buy these shares with a specific aim to get him out of work, using money as a tool to give him the life he wanted but bought them as a method of saving up as much money as he could.

By the age of 63, he had 72,000 shares worth around €17 each (well over €1 million at their peak) and a pension from his job. However, he never spent any of this and lived on the money he earned from the consultancy work he began immediately after retiring. He lived until 69, but in constant pain and discomfort. I often wondered how much better his life would have been if he'd cashed in some of his shares.

Mark

At the age of 25, in the 1960's, Mark inherited a fortune. At that time it was sufficient to buy 20 nice houses in London or New York. Instead, he bought one house to live in and eked out the rest of the money over 50 years.

Too frightened to spend it, he lived in abject poverty, never heating his house or paying for repairs. Had he bought houses or built businesses that generated an income with the cash instead of eking out the capital, how different would his life have been?

Finbarr

Finbarr had an enormous amount of savings and shares. He had a great house, worth a fortune, in a fantastic location and also a very high-paying job. He saved half his income every month and the family spent the rest on living costs.

However, his house was so shabby and down-at-heel it was shocking! Nothing was ever replaced or mended because he was too frightened to spend any money. Ancient sofas were held together with duct tape. He felt he could not afford to pay for his children's education, so they had to make do with the local sink school. His wife gave up and stopped cleaning and tidying the house, saying, "Give me a house to be proud of and I'll become house-proud."

The theme …

The theme here seems to be: very good at saving, comparing rates, setting up automatic accounts, but not good at leveraging. Those with a *Comfortable* mindset will invest in what they see as safe vehicles. They don't like risk. However the risk of holding cash or shares without a good exit strategy can very often lead to loss of money.

For example, savings held in times of low interest or high inflation lose value, or shares bought without a time-frame to sell may lose value or not be reinvested to maximise wealth building. Money invested in a pension can be worth very little by the time it is needed.

This was the way that my dad behaved with his shares – he never cashed them in, never spent any of the financial gain from them, had no exit strategy, nor any plan to further invest the money or use it in any way, except to save for a rainy day. He just kept buying and holding them, enjoying the feeling of security that it gave him.

He watched the value go up and up yet still went to a job he loathed every day. When he finally did retire through ill-health, he was far too physically wrecked to enjoy his boat or garden even though he had a fortune locked up in the shares. His entire retirement was spent hobbling about, bent double, on medication, in agony.

Even so, he worked part-time as a consultant throughout his retirement. Unable to walk, he would sit in his clients' premises and they would bring to him all he needed to make decisions and give advice.

He lived off this consultancy income and saved his pension. Seeing someone who hated every second of his working life leave himself with such a poor quality of life after finishing work was pitiful. Furthermore, he saved his pension, refusing to replace the crumbling windows or kitchen in his house. He saved every penny he could and spent only a small amount on living costs. This was his pattern: save huge amounts for security, give a designated portion and live on whatever was left.

The Structure of the Comfortable Money Mindset

Below are 10 working examples of the *Comfortable Money Mindset*. Again read each one carefully to see what resonates with you and what doesn't. Note the comments in the *Beliefs, Values, Feelings, Thoughts, Decisions, Actions* and *Results* boxes are actual client responses.

Example 1

Beliefs	My financial security is my responsibility
Values	The Lord helps those who help themselves
	I must ensure my financial security
Feelings	Threat/insecurity
	Feel secure with big savings
	Feel secure with no debts

Thoughts	People who save are responsible I must save for a rainy day
Decisions	Focussed around financial security Alert to financial threats Least risk
Actions	Minimise risk Save
Results	Big savings Low risk investments

Example 2

Beliefs	Big savings give security
Values	It is vitally important to save One should save a proportion of all money that comes in It is easy to save
Feelings	Feel safe with savings Feel protected from financial uncertainties with large savings Feel insecure if savings drop below a certain level Feel control / power by being able to defer gratification
Thoughts	It is easy to save Frequently thinks about savings
Decisions	Saving is a priority Only spend what is left even if I have to do without Would never blow savings
Actions	Save first Resist spending Do not spend if it can be avoided
Results	Outgoings always smaller than income

Example 3

Beliefs	Debt is a threat, sometimes necessary but always a threat to security
Values	I never take on too much debt It is wrong to borrow for anything except a house
Feelings	Fear of debt
Thoughts	Keep any debts from becoming a risk
Decisions	Prevent excessive debt
Actions	No borrowings, only mortgages
Results	Low debts Wealth grows very slowly

Example 4

Beliefs	Money is safety
Values	When I need some more, I do without something so I can save more
Feelings	Fear Feel better by spending very little
Thoughts	I must find ways to save money and stop spending when the in-flow of money is low
Decisions	Always save more when I see threats
Actions	Only spend on absolute necessities
Results	Flow becomes less

Example 5

Beliefs	You can lose very badly by taking financial risk
Values	Only risk what you can afford to lose
Feelings	I feel secure with safe investments I feel threatened by risk
Thoughts	I evaluate investments and make sure they are safe
Decisions	Only choose low risk investments
Actions	Low risk choices

Results	Very rarely loses any money, wealth grows very slowly

Example 6

Beliefs	There are many financial threats/dangers to protect yourself against
Values	It is important to understand how current and future events will cause financial problems in the future
Feelings	Feel fear at future financial insecurity Panic at direct financial threats
Thoughts	Plans to combat how current events will cause/ could cause financial problems in the future
Decisions	Keep threats away Minimise dangers
Actions	Work for money
Results	Surroundings often do not reflect the money they have

Example 7

Beliefs	People who take big financial risks and lose deserve what they get. They could lose everything
Values	Be the tortoise not the hare when it comes to building wealth
Feelings	Worry that events might cause future financial loss/catastrophe
Thoughts	I think of ways to build my wealth without risk of losing it
Decisions	Keep threats away Minimise dangers
Actions	Make very cautious financial decisions
Results	Sells time for money Makes more money by working harder or longer hours

Example 8

Beliefs	People who get into debt and find they cannot pay it back are irresponsible
Values	People who don't save and defer gratification are not only lazy but careless
Feelings	Resent those who pass financial responsibility onto others
Thoughts	Even though I take financial responsibility there are many who pass it to others
Decisions	Always save and do without in order to save
Actions	Save money
Results	Money tied up (pensions, investment vehicles, high interest accounts etc) – not available for use

Example 9

Beliefs	I will never spend my financial cushion
Values	Those with no savings are mad I could never be without savings, ever
Feelings	Fear of being without money in the future Need certainty
Thoughts	I understand financial risk I will do everything to hang on to my savings
Decisions	Never part with much money
Actions	Scrimp and save
Results	Big savings but no real plan on what to use money and savings for

Example 10

Beliefs	Sometimes you have to do things you don't like to earn money I could never just give up my job, no matter how much I hate it, unless I had a very big financial cushion
Values	People just have to suck it up and get on with it even if they don't like it People who pack in their jobs are mad
Feelings	Feel like I have no choice
Thoughts	How do I make it easier? How do I get through the day?
Decisions	Decide I have no choice
Actions	Stick at job Make myself go in to work
Results	Works for money Sticks at/spends years at jobs they hate

Once again, review this section carefully because this is based on a good cross-section of comfortable client case studies - people who save money, create buffers and avoid anything that threatens financial stability.

If *Comfortable* sounds most like you, then you may even construct a sample grid of the comments from the various examples to compile a more personalised *Comfortable* chart.

If this sounds like you, I also suggest you go back and reread the *Rich* money mindset.

Money Mindset 3 – Break-Even

Those who habitually run a *Break-even* money mindset are driven to cover their expenses and spend the rest.

They pay all the fixed expenses first then spend what is left on variable expenses, but do not spend more than they have. If they run out of money they stop spending, believing that once it's gone, it's gone. They would never take on debt.

The pattern seen in their bank statements is one of running out of money by the end of the payment period. Savings are for specific items or events.

In response to my Key Questions a clear pattern of actions specific to the break-even money mindset emerges:

- Spend
- Give
- Save

They tend to cover their expenses, rent and bills first and spend the rest. They then will give to family and friends through presents and treats. Finally, whatever is left over they save for something specific.

This mindset does exactly what it says on the tin.

People with this mindset prioritise their spending, allocate money and stop spending when the money is gone. They save what is left over for a specific item or purpose. Some with this mindset are very good at current account budgeting and sometimes budget using the envelope system.

Examples of the Break-Even Money Mindset
My grandmother

My maternal grandmother believed that to be successful with money, people had to feed themselves, pay their bills, keep the roof over their heads and not get into debt.

She did not have a bank account, as she believed such things were instruments of the rich (and the devil), and managed her money in three jars – one for bills, one for food and the third for upcoming expenses.

Every week was the same: 1. Spend; 2.Give; 3. Save what was left (but this never lasted long).

Auntie Eva

Auntie Eva had the same mindset. She abhorred debt and had a saying: 'neither a borrower nor a lender be'. She lived on a modest widow's pension, adored travel and always had enough money for trips. She spent on essentials, took friends out to lunch, bought gifts and saved the rest to fund holidays. She never had any long term savings. When she died there was just enough to cover her funeral.

Vera

My neighbour, Vera, lived on a very modest income and loved to be financially organised; she had numerous spreadsheets to help her prioritise her spending.

"I have always been good with money and have never been in debt in my life. I studied accountancy after I left school and love to balance the books. I have spreadsheets to ensure everything reconciles."

She balanced her books every month, always paying all her bills and expenses first. Then she would give to her grandchildren. Whenever she had a little left over she would save it. Then though, her son would get into debt and guilt-trip Vera into bailing him out every time. I lived near her for over a decade and saw this pattern acted out regularly with total predictability.

The Structure of the Break-Even Money Mindset

Below are 11 working examples of the *Break-Even Money Mindset*. Read each example carefully to see if this money mindset resonates with you or not. Note again that the comments in the *Beliefs, Values, Feelings, Thoughts, Decisions, Actions* and *Results* boxes are actual client responses.

Example 1

Beliefs	People who pay all their bills on time are good with money
Values	Because I pay all my bills on time, I am good with money
Feelings	I feel free to spend what's left
Thoughts	I prefer my bills to be paid first so I don't have to think / worry about them
Decisions	Pay all bills / costs first and spend what's left
Actions	Cover expenses, spend the rest freely
Results	Bills are always up to date

Example 2

Beliefs	Debt is bad
Values	I take pride in never being in debt
Feelings	Uneasy with debt
Thoughts	Debt is very bad
Decisions	Make do with what I have
Actions	Cover all my expenses first, so I never owe anyone anything
Results	Never in debt

Example 3

Beliefs	People who get into debt are not good with money
Values	Neither a borrower nor a lender be
Feelings	I would feel sick at the thought of owing money
Thoughts	Make sure they pay their expenses first
Decisions	Don't lend money to people who won't repay
Actions	Hang about with similar people
Results	Current account balanced

Example 4

Beliefs	When I don't have enough money I wait for more to come in
Values	It's good to be able to wait until I can afford something, not borrow for it
Feelings	I feel good about being able to wait until I have the money
Thoughts	Even if I really need something I know how to get by until my money comes in without borrowing
Decisions	Wait
Actions	Make do until my money comes in
Results	No debt

Example 5

Beliefs	I successfully save for specific items/events
Values	I am good at putting away money for something specific
Feelings	I feel good when my saving plan is on target for something I need/want
Thoughts	I plan ahead what I need money for and make sure I save for it
Decisions	Choose what to save for and what to spend on
Actions	Buy what I have saved for
Results	Buy what I need without getting into any debt

Example 6

Beliefs	If I have a bit of surplus money left over I try to save it, but something always happens that requires me to spend any surplus
Values	If I have some savings and there is an emergency, I need to use them
Feelings	I must sort the situation out using my savings
Thoughts	Something has happened; I need to use my savings
Decisions	I will use my savings
Actions	Spend savings
Results	Never have surplus money/savings for long

Example 7

Beliefs	People like us/me never get rich
Values	I'm not important enough to be rich
Feelings	I feel a bit hopeless; I have never had a lot of money and never will Feel desperate
Thoughts	I have enough to live on and that's enough
Decisions	Decide to stay poor I'm fine as I am
Actions	Give up on myself, never take the actions I need to
Results	Stays breaking even financially

Example 8

Beliefs	It is very hard to hang on to savings
Values	It is very hard for an ordinary person to get rich
Feelings	Want to feel in control Want to feel organised
Thoughts	How should I prioritise?
Decisions	Prioritise expenditure
Actions	Budget
Results	Never in debt

Example 9

Beliefs	I successfully save for specific items/events
Values	I am good at putting away money for something specific
Feelings	I feel good when my saving plan is on target for something I need/want
Thoughts	I plan ahead what I need money for and make sure I save for it
Decisions	Choose what to save for and what to spend on
Actions	Buy what I have saved for
Results	Buy what I need without getting into any debt

Example 10

Beliefs	Rich people are lucky Rich people have money so they can always spend what they want
Values	I'm not going to be rich
Feelings	Frustration Envy rich people
Thoughts	Rich people don't have to worry about money; they can do whatever they feel like Having money is so easy for them
Decisions	Live within means
Actions	Find it impossible to keep any surplus money for long
Results	Break-even

Example 11

Beliefs	Poor people don't understand money, spend beyond their means and get into debt
Values	I make sure I do not become poor
Feelings	I would feel uncomfortable if I couldn't pay a bill
Thoughts	I understand money. I plan and budget
Decisions	Live within your means
Actions	Never spend what you don't have
Results	Never in debt

Once again, review this section carefully.

Money Mindset 4 – In-Debt

Those who habitually run an *In-Debt* money mindset are driven to borrow and spend. They have already spent some or all of their money by the time they get it.

This pattern shows up in their bank statements as money coming in then immediately going out to meet debt commitments such as car loans, bank loans, credit and store card loans or loans to friends or family.

Someone running an *In-debt* money mindset habitually thinks, feels and says to himself and everyone around him that he hasn't got enough money. He often finds himself driven by a feeling of 'not enough' or lack. In response to this habitual feeling, he often finds himself spending to feel better.

In response to my Key Questions a clear pattern of actions specific to the *In-debt* money mindset emerges:

- Borrow
- Give
- Spend

This mindset is exactly what it describes. Those with an *In-Debt* mindset find that as soon as they get money in, a portion of it is immediately swallowed by debt, further fuelling the feeling of 'never enough money', as is so characteristic of this mindset. Often people go on like this for years because they 'manage' the debt and their income is sufficient to cover it. Sometimes, though, life gets in the way, they lose their income and then lose control of the debt.

Examples of the In-Debt Money Mindset

Margaret

Margaret brought up her child on her own without any support from the father. She permanently felt resentful and lacking money. She borrowed money from anywhere she could – bank, credit cards and family and took every penny of her mother's pension. When her mother signed her house over to Margaret, it was remortgaged within two months. When she did get some money she spent it on holidays and clothes to make herself feel better.

She was never out of debt throughout her adult life.

Myra

Myra explained: "Feeling deprived in so many areas as a child meant that I did the opposite with my kids. They always have whatever they want, regardless of whether I can afford it and regardless of whether it is good for them, or if the money could have been spent on something better, because I don't want them to feel deprived as I did.

Whenever I haven't been able to buy what they want, I feel like a terrible mother, and have dreadful guilt. I still feel they don't get enough. No matter how stretched my finances are I will find a way of getting the money to give my kids whatever they want. As soon as I have any money, some of it is grabbed away for debt payments.

I spend what I have on my children then borrow whatever I can. I don't want to be in debt but I just don't have enough money."

The Structure of the In-Debt Money Mindset

Below are 10 working examples of the *In-Debt* money mindset. Read each example very carefully to see if this money mindset feels like you. Understand, clients who are typically stuck in this mindset often feel defensive about being labelled *In-Debt* and can defend and justify this mindset vigorously with good reasons and excuses. Stay open-minded as you read on.

Example 1

Beliefs	When I need something and I don't have the money, I have to borrow
Values	It is important for me to be able to borrow if I really want /need something
Feelings	Resignation/acceptance of situation
Thoughts	I have to have (something particular); the only way I can get it is to borrow
Decisions	Determined to find a way of borrowing the money
Actions	Borrow money
Results	In-Debt

Example 2

Beliefs	If I had more money I would not need to borrow
Values	If I had more money I would always have enough
Feelings	Resentment, guilt and shame
Thoughts	If I had more money everything would be OK
Decisions	I must/have to get more

Actions	Borrow more money Spend
Results	Panic because of fear of debt

Example 3

Beliefs	People find themselves without enough money because of bad luck or injustice
Values	Life is unfair
Feelings	Resentment, acceptance and apathy
Thoughts	It ought not to be so unfair There nothing I can do about my lack of money, it's all down to chance, who you are and what you are born with
Decisions	Give up
Actions	Borrow and spend
Results	Debt

Example 4

Beliefs	It is unfair so many have more than me
Values	It's important me that my kids don't have to have less than others
Feelings	Shame Self-pity Envy Anger / frustration Sadness
Thoughts	Why should me and my kids have less than everyone else?
Decisions	I will buy what we need
Actions	Spend
Results	Guilt for spending and guilt for not having enough Never able to get sorted

Example 5

Beliefs	Rich people are lucky; they can spend whatever they want, whenever they want
Values	It's easy for them, they always have plenty of money, they don't know what it's like
Feelings	Anger / frustration Self-pity Resentment
Thoughts	They never have to think about money. They should understand what it's like for the rest of us
Decisions	Choose to believe that rich people are different from the rest of us – don't like rich people
Actions	Act in ways that are 'anti-rich' Say and do things that are 'anti-rich'
Results	Persecute rich people

Example 6

Beliefs	Something / someone is causing me not to have enough money
Values	People like me have to borrow to get the things we desperately need
Feelings	Everything is getting on top of me I'm so anxious Shame
Thoughts	It's easy for others who have more It's too much I try desperately not to think about it
Decisions	Indecision Denial
Actions	Put bills in drawer Ignore them
Results	Deeper in debt Despair

Example 7

Beliefs	If I had more money people would look up to me
Values	I should be able to have what I need and want
Feelings	I'm ashamed because I'm in debt I'm ashamed to say I can't afford something
Thoughts	It will be OK. I'll manage to pay it all back
Decisions	I have to buy it
Actions	Buy it
Results	More debt

Example 8

Beliefs	If I had more symbols of wealth I'd be happier
Values	It is important for me to have all the outward signs of financial success
Feelings	Buzz from spending
Thoughts	I need these things to be accepted
Decisions	I will get things that symbolise wealth, even if I can't afford them
Actions	Spend when already in debt Borrow to pay for clothes, cars, holidays, entertainment, gifts, etc.
Results	Things that need to be paid for each month

Example 9

Beliefs	I have to have it now
Values	I will get it regardless
Feelings	I feel good when I spend
Thoughts	I deserve a treat/break
Decisions	I will spend
Actions	Lie about purchases, self deception
Results	Poor credit rating, credit risk

Example 10

Beliefs	I must have (certain things)
Values	It is vitally important that I get this
Feelings	Power from spending Competitiveness / keeping up with the Joneses
Thoughts	How can I *borrow* money?
Decisions	I will try anyone / anything I can to get the money as quickly as possible
Actions	Borrow money from friends / family
Results	Falling out with people Lost friendships because of unpaid loans

Review this section several times because this is based on feedback of a large cross-section of in-debt client case studies.

If *In-Debt* sounds most like you make a note of the exact characteristics that sound exactly like you and then read on.

You can change this mindset and contrary to whatever you think or feel it is not set in stone and you are not permanently locked in. Anyone can snap out of this mindset at anytime.

Action Steps

Recognising Money Mindset Behaviours

Learn to recognise the behaviours of all four money mindsets. I suggest you reread the four money mindsets several times and get a real sense of what sounds like you. Maybe you already know.

Chapter 6

What is Your Default Money Mindset?

Have you identified your money mindset yet?

Because of our money mindsets, we all have a 'financial default position'. This means that even if our financial position changes and we get an unexpected sum of money, or lose money, we will with time revert back to that default financial position. Most of us will have seen this happen and maybe even experienced it ourselves.

Think of someone you know who is very rich, for example, Richard Branson. What do you think his default financial position might be?

If Richard Branson lost everything he owned, would he have above or below the average amount of money (taking the average UK income of £26,500 in 2015) three years later? Why?

An example of the financial default position in action is the Ugandan Asians expelled from their homeland in 1972 with nothing, who went on to build back up all their wealth in one generation.

The Ugandan Government, under President Idi Amin, gave all Ugandan Asians exactly 90 days to leave the country accusing them of taking wealth from native

Ugandans, hoarding it and sabotaging the economy. The Asians in Uganda had been extremely financially successful and had a significant influence on the Ugandan economy; they constituted one percent of the population but controlled a fifth of the national income.

President Amin wanted to return that wealth to the ordinary Ugandan people. In August 1972, Amin gave the Ugandan Asians ninety days to leave the country, forcing more than 70,000 people to leave behind highly successful businesses as well as their homes. The Ugandan Government stripped them of everything they owned, and they fled with nothing but £50 each. Many tried to enter Britain.

Britain eventually agreed to allow entry to some of these deportees after a great deal of hostility.

The Leicester City Council took out a now infamous advert in a widely-read Uganda Argus newspaper warning migrants against going to Leicester as no housing, schools or health services would be available for them.

27,000 Ugandan Asians did, however, come to the UK, with nothing but whatever they had managed to smuggle out of Uganda and their £50. From the moment they arrived and settled they began to rebuild. Bit by bit they succeeded. Within a single generation these people had started and built successful businesses and sent their children to university. Forty years later, they are once again financially successful.

A generation later the Ugandan government tried to entice back some of those citizens they had expelled, finally recognising that they had played a key role in the country's wealth generation. Clearly they were more than just greedy people hoarding all the money and keeping it for themselves: they were people who took actions that resulted in wealth creation. This was their *Rich* money mindset at work.

Paul Harris, writing on the 30th anniversary for the Observer newspaper in 2002, relates the success story of the Ugandan Asians who arrived in Britain in 1972 says that most arrived with nothing. Thirty years on, despite being told they were unwelcome, they have flourished and have become Britain's most successful immigrant community.

In politics Shailesh Vara is now Parliamentary Under Secretary of State at the Department of Work and Pensions and the Ministry of Justice. Lata Patel was Mayor of Brent. In the media Yasmin Alibhai-Brown is one of Britain's most distinguished columnists. Asif Din was an accomplished Warwickshire cricketer, while Tarique Ghaffur was the deputy assistant commissioner of the Metropolitan Police. Industrialist, Manubhai Madhvani was worth £160 million in 2002.

It's estimated that their businesses have created over 30,000 jobs in the Leicester region.

We all have a default money mindset position. And we automatically revert to type. You absorbed this mindset from your parents and the key people around you.

Your financial situation is a direct reflection of your beliefs and values about money. Those beliefs and values form an underlying force that drives your financial results.

We know that poor people have a very tough time and face terrible challenges and situations because of lack of money. When working as a debt adviser I found many of my clients' experiences to be heart wrenching. But giving money alone to a poor person may not eliminate their poverty in the longer term. Two people, each with the same amount of money, may experience either poverty or wealth.

The same is true for time management. Everyone has exactly the same amount of time in the day.

Some people consistently experience time poverty while others seem to have enough time to do what they need. If you could give someone who experiences time poverty an extra bit of time in the day, do you think it would make a big difference to them? Probably not, because this is all about their perception of 'enough' time and how they manage their time in the first place.

So it's evident that something deeper drives financial results. The first time I noticed this was when I saw what happened to the money in my immediate family.

My father, who was a generous and caring man, repeatedly recreated conditions of poverty and lack in his and our family's lives over and over again through his fear; by being too afraid to follow his dream and set up a fishing equipment shop; too afraid to quit a job that destroyed him; too afraid to let my mother retire early from a job she hated; too afraid to sell shares and live with ease. He was simply too afraid to change.

When I was around three, my father had set up a business growing and supplying vegetables to shops; he then expanded to selling hair accessories as well. This business failed about three years later, as most first-time small businesses do.

My great grandfather, who founded a hugely successful chain of department stores, failed twice in business before he got it right. Years later, the same happened with one of my businesses too, so I understand how difficult it is to get back in the saddle.

For the first 18 months after Dad's business folded, he stayed out in his fishing boat, smoking endless cigarettes, in a state of complete shock and denial. The bank manager threatened to repossess our home. Mum went back to work as a teacher and carried on in that job for the next 30 years, loathing every single day.

I don't think I recall ever seeing her happy. Dad took a job in another of the family's businesses and also worked for 30 years in a job that he hated with every fibre of his being.

The Drama Behind the Mindset

There is a saying: *"You do everything the way you do money,"* which means that how you behave with money, is how you behave about all aspects of your life.

Some of us may already be familiar with the *Karpman Drama Triangle*, developed by Dr Steven B Karpman MD in 1968.

The basic concept underpinning the *Karpman Drama Triangle* is the connection between responsibility, power and vulnerability between people, particularly in how they feel about themselves in relation to others.

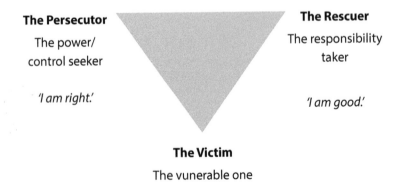

The Persecutor

The power/
control seeker

'I am right.'

The Rescuer

The responsibility
taker

'I am good.'

The Victim

The vunerable one

'I am blameless and I need to be looked after.'

Each position on this triangle has unique, readily identifiable characteristics. Individuals may have a default position – that is, one they adopt much of the time – but where there is dysfunctional behaviour they tend to spin from role to role around this triangle.

The Victim

Victims believe they are vulnerable and have no power or responsibility. Their mistreatment and suffering forms their identity. Things are never right and there is never enough. They always need something 'more' before they are willing to take responsibility for their life and take any action. They always have a reason for inaction.

Indifference, depression and anger are characteristic states. No matter how much energy, information, time or support you provide victims, they rarely change.

The Rescuer

Rescuers believe they have a responsibility to 'care' for those not capable of caring for themselves, that is victims. They believe they have all the answers and know the right solutions for others.

Through controlling and changing others they attempt to get a sense of identity as well as attention and respect. But through taking that responsibility away from other individuals, they render them powerless. They spend their time taking care of and directing others' lives, but their own life might be a mess. Without someone, something or a cause to 'rescue', the rescuer feels lost, no longer the knight in shining armour, the liberator or protector – and can end up aimless and even jobless without someone to rescue.

The Persecutor

Persecutors blame others for their own negative feelings, and punish others through destructive actions. They are harshly judgemental, often motivated by a fear of loss of control, and can be extremely unempathetic and unfeeling towards others' incompetence or suffering.

The Cycle in Action

Person A borrows money from person B; person C is a colleague of both.

A is short of money (and feels he has no responsibility for this). B feels sorry for him (and feels responsible for helping him financially because A is his friend), and lends him a significant sum of money after A fervently promises to repay it.

A then cannot repay (and feels no responsibility for this either); he simply does not have enough. B needs the money back urgently, as he now cannot pay his rent, and complains bitterly to C, who (feeling responsible for helping his friend B) has an argument with A, pointing out that it's A's fault that B can't pay his rent.

A, feeling aggrieved, has an argument with B, blaming him for motivating C to verbally attack him.

C then feels that A and B have ganged up on him and the whole situation is hopeless and tells his boss what's happened and that he wants to move to another department.

Where people have a dysfunction in the way they relate to the rest of the world, it also shows up in the actions they take with money, whether their own or someone else's.

Look at what someone you know does with money. Are they mostly a rescuer, persecutor or victim? They will also behave this way in other aspects of their life.

Who a person is on the inside shows up in how they are with money. Money, or lack of it is not the cause of their behaviour. Money is the great revealer.

You will see a persecutor when you spot one, take money unfairly or punish others for their incompetence.

A rescuer will want access to more and more money, so that they can rescue more people – regardless of whether it would serve those people in the long run or not.

A victim wants to be given more and more, because they will always need rescuing.

Money Makes You More of What You Are

By way of example, here are some very rich people who show very different behaviours with money: Richard Branson, Bob Geldof, Bill and Melinda Gates, Robert Mugabe, Justin Bieber, Katie Price, Bernie Madoff, Wayne Rooney.

If you are operating in one of these dysfunctional roles you will be running beliefs that will lead to negative financial results in your life.

If you believe you are financially vulnerable, have no power or responsibility and need to be rescued, you will have poor financial results. If you believe others need to be rescued, you are imposing what you think is right for them. They will have poor financial results and not learn how to run their own finances, consequently ending up in a poverty trap where they continually need rescuing. If you blame others for their financial problems or poverty instead of behaving with compassion and generosity, you make decisions that keep other people poor.

With any of these dysfunctions you are keeping yourself or others in old limiting mindsets that stop them choosing different, more helpful beliefs that would make their financial lives better.

We can relate these dysfunctions back to the money mindsets. Let's recap some of the core beliefs.

In-Debt

- There is never enough.
- It's not my fault, I am blameless.
- I am powerless around money.
- Someone/something should/will rescue me.

Break-Even

- Those who get into debt are bad with money.
- It upsets me when I always have to pay for people who are bad with money.
- Rich people are bad and take advantage of the poor.

Comfortable

- People who get into debt deserve what happens to them. Why should others have to give them handouts?
- People who don't take care of their financial security deserve what happens as a result.
- I'm not paying for people who have not taken care of their money.
- You should not risk anything you cannot afford to lose.

Any of these roles can stop you developing a rich money mindset.

Real Life Examples

Feeling like victims, my parents came to bitterly resent the self-employed because business owners were able to avoid many of the stringent taxes my parents had to pay, which meant that they felt very poor even though both had good jobs. They also resented welfare recipients who, at that time in Ireland, had free dental and medical care, help with university fees, etc, while regular employees, who paid high taxes, still had to pay for every service.

One man who lived near us was a school headmaster. The only way he could afford for all five of his children to go to university was to give up his job and go on welfare, because that way, they would all be eligible for a grant. My mother had to choose between dental care for herself and university fees for us. She let her teeth rot.

The default position shows up when an individual is under pressure. Then, you can easily spot money patterns. You see these as soon as they:

- Are short of money
- Get any money
- Need to make a financial decision.

They are working to a model or pattern.

The Victim

A financial victim believes that an external cause or event is responsible for their financial position; that they are completely blameless for any problems they have with money. You might observe someone with the money victim pattern blaming financial circumstances or lack of money on others, specific or general. For example, they will say things like, "I don't have enough money because of the government," or "... because rich people have taken it all," or "My job doesn't pay enough."

It is not only poor people from deprived areas who believe they are financial victims. I have seen many middle-class people with plenty of financial resources and opportunities behaving like victims; people who loathe their jobs but continue to sit and wait, sometimes for decades, for a redundancy pay-off, or keep working solely to get a pension. They waste the most precious resource they have – time – being financial victims who, deep down, believe the only way they would generate a large sum of money is by getting a pay-off to leave their hated job.

The most desperate situation I remember was the case of a talented and brilliant man who approached the world from a place of fear. That fear caused him to behave like a financial victim.

He had asked a manager in his organisation (who had no understanding of finances) for financial advice but her advice was incorrect. He lost the opportunity to gain a significant additional income stream, which, I think, caused him to feel more fearful and vulnerable.

He waited, hating his job, until his late fifties for the pay-off. He spent a decade waiting for that event, then when he finally received the money, stuck the whole lot in the bank and lived off a very modest income rather than using it as a tool to take him to the next level as he had originally wanted. The last I heard, he was nearing 60 and waiting for his father's death so he could inherit and start to invest in property.

A guy I know wanted to invest in property for a pension, so he bought some houses that barely put any money in his pocket after expenses. His rationale was that they would make him money in the future (whenever that might be). This man is intelligent and creative but, because he follows the pattern of a financial victim, he spends the majority of his time working for an organisation he dislikes. Such a waste of wonderful human potential, just because of seeing the world through the eyes of a victim! I told him that I too had considered property as a pension but with a view to creating a pension now rather than in the future.

That meant my property purchase decisions were much better and more focused on creating an income in the present.

Some people feel that all their problems in life are caused by lack of money. They say things like: *"I had to give it away to my children"*; *"I don't earn enough"*; *"My parents wouldn't give it to me"*; *"Rich people have taken it all and there's not enough to go round."* All these things might be true, but if you continue to believe them, you are giving away all the power that you have to be able to generate money for yourself.

We have all felt and behaved like financial victims at one time or another. We have all blamed others or external circumstances for the poor state of our finances.

Sarah, a lady I knew well, struggled terribly for money throughout her life. Because of this struggle, she believed that any actions around money, no matter how bad, were justifiable.

She stole from a charity and explicitly overturned her aunt's dying wish about the nature of her burial so she could profit. And while the elderly aunt was dying in hospital, Sarah stripped the old lady's house of every single belonging, hiring vans to remove everything.

The Rescuer

A financial rescuer considers that they are virtuous and righteous in their beliefs and behaviour with money. Rescuers might find themselves taking financial responsibility for others, perhaps by paying for what someone else should take responsibility for.

Barbara's grown-up daughter, Joy, regularly spent her income on holidays and clothes and when she was threatened with having her gas and electricity cut off, Barbara always picked up the bills.

Joy, therefore, never took financial responsibility for herself. This pattern got worse when Joy had children.

Barbara was continually pressured to buy essentials for the children, which she always did even though she had very little money. On a few occasions when Barbara was with me, she cried because she found the stress of finding money to bail out her daughter overwhelming. She lamented over why Joy would not grow up and take responsibility at the age of 38.

Barbara had been financially independent since she was 16. Sadly, Barbara died suddenly. Without her rescuer Joy was forced to look for another. She immediately married someone she didn't respect or love to support her continued spending. Joy fell into the habit of complaining bitterly to anyone who would listen how unfair it was that she had to tolerate being with her husband because she needed his money.

There are many ways that someone can play the role of financial rescuer. One of the most common situations is where one family member takes financial responsibility for someone in the same family unit, be they a grown-up child or another adult.

Similarly, where a financial rescuer is operating, children are rarely taught to take financial responsibility.

Mary's 25 year old son, Adam, lives rent free in a large house owned by his mother. While Mary lives in a small city flat, working 15 hours a day on renovating a block of flats to produce an income, Adam has no job and shows no sign of being prepared to do anything to take financial responsibility for himself. But Mary is reluctant to stop taking financial responsibility for her son and it is obvious that until she stops supporting him, Adam will not start being responsible.

One day she explained what was really behind the situation. When Adam was 14, Mary and her husband split up. That year, Adam did very badly at school and failed all his exams. Mary blamed herself and felt guilty and has continued to feel responsible for all of Adam's failures ever since.

Ideally Mary, in a kind and compassionate way, needs to let Adam understand that we as adult individuals are responsible for everything that happens in our lives. Only we can find our own solutions. Taking responsibility away from someone else for what truly belongs to them is taking away the possibility of them being able to build the life they want.

In society, this is evident where financial help is not just a temporary support until someone can get back on their feet, but a belief that it is someone's fault that poor people are poor; and so the state must permanently 'rescue' them because they are powerless to ever take any financial responsibility for themselves. Entire workforces are dedicated to maintaining and rescuing the poor and confirming all their beliefs that vast swathes of people can only survive on state aid.

Some vulnerable people are genuinely not able to take responsibility for themselves and so will need state aid for their entire life. A society that values sustaining those too vulnerable to sustain themselves will always support those in need. A society, however, that believes that poverty is someone else's fault and not the individual's responsibility, will rescue rather than enable.

Ideally, far more focus should be given to educating people born in poverty to the lessons learned by those born with wealth. If a poor person is only exposed to a *Poor* money mindset, how will they take back their power and prosper? We must begin to empower rather than persecute or rescue people.

What might happen if we exposed all schoolchildren to the lessons of creating wealth so they could live the lives they want, rather than educating them to conform to the *Poor* money mindset?

The Persecutor

If:

- you believe your views about money are right, and people who hold other views are wrong
- you consider your views on who deserves or does not deserve money to be right
- you feel smug about your financial position
- you feel very little compassion for people who make poor financial decisions and believe they get what they deserve

… then you are a financial persecutor.

An individual driven by a sense of power from getting one over other people, or from making them do exactly as he wants because he is controlling the money, is a financial bully. The golden rule of the financial bully is: 'He who has the gold makes the rules'.

Persecutors use others' perceived vulnerability around money to bully them. They have beliefs about poor people they use to justify their behaviour. Some attack the rich and blame them for the ills of society. When it comes to financial persecution, it doesn't seem to matter whether the object of attack is rich or poor.

For example, one of the persecutor's set of beliefs and thoughts about the poor are likely to be that they are feckless and lazy, and that all our financial problems are caused by an underclass sponging off the state; immigrants and single parents, they complain, are dragging the country to ruin.

My paternal grandfather truly believed that all economic woes should be laid at the feet of a group of people called 'the workers'. My Auntie Beccy, who was very wealthy and used numerous accountants to ensure she paid as little tax as possible, was known to shake with anger when she spoke of those on welfare: "They are living off us, the parasites!" She had convinced herself that the poor were living entirely at the expense of herself and others like her.

My maternal grandmother, on the other hand, held deep-set persecutor beliefs towards the rich. She loved any laws that would extract money from them, and held the view that they should be stripped of all of their wealth and horse-whipped in the streets! She believed that the only good rich person was a dead rich person, because 'they' took the money from the poor. 'They' were the ones who owned the means of production, and kept the poor in poverty within these demonic factories.

I remember when I was about nine, the supermarket across from Granny's house was robbed. She had watched the entire event from her window. When the police called to make enquiries, Granny was adamant she saw nothing. I was shocked and asked her why she did this. She said, "Never ever under any circumstance tell the police about any crime because all they would do is beat the perpetrators senseless." This was Granny's reality.

Neither of these groups – rich or poor – are the cause of all of society's ills. Greedy and evil people can be found in all financial groups.

A pimp from grinding poverty in Eastern Europe who is trafficking children for prostitution is no more or less evil than a wealthy American pimp.

Corporate fraud is no less or more serious in its intention than benefit fraud. To believe this stops us taking responsibility for the actions, caused by our own beliefs, that lead to our results.

It is said that money makes you more of what you are. The more you have, the more it enables you to be what you are. If you are a giver, it will provide you with the means to give more. If you are a taker, it will provide you with greater power to take more.

Over 30 years ago I saw an extreme version of a taker/ persecutor with money, who used his power to take too much.

My brother Ralph was 13 at the time and wanted to earn some money. He got a shovel and a bucket and went from door to door where we lived in Cork, looking for gardening work. He did several little jobs for people and was very happy.

Then one day a man up the road agreed that he could dig the whole of his large and overgrown garden for £13. (I was working as a shop girl at this point, and earning about £80 a week.) Ralph very soon discovered he had seriously undercharged for the job, but the homeowner made him stick to his word. Ralph spent over two weeks digging the garden, coming home blistered and exhausted every evening. That homeowner certainly taught Ralph a valuable lesson in how to recognise financial bullies who exploit financial weakness.

Some people use money to persecute others in a dishonourable manner. I heard a man proudly boast to his friends that he had a young learning disabled man do his garden for him on a regular basis. This young man didn't understand money so the man systematically paid him about 5% of the going rate for the job. He did this and got away with it because he was in a position of power.

Another person I knew used his financial power over others with poorer money mindsets. He paid his staff as little as he could and took every opportunity not to pay them at all. Once, when there was a three-day holiday for a Royal wedding, he refused to pay his staff because the enforced bank holiday meant they had to have the day off. The people who stayed with him were the fearful victims. He played underhand, committing financial offences and cheating people.

Luke moved into a small village where many of the locals had limited means, travelled very little and lived modestly. Luke, whose father was a multi-millionaire, travelled around the world staying in five-star hotels and was used to the good things in life.

Wanting to support local businesses, he commissioned a local builder to build and install a magnificent kitchen in his house. This kitchen was like nothing that Luke's village neighbours had ever seen or heard of in their lives; few of them had even seen the magazines that advertised this type of kitchen. He went away on an exotic holiday for a number of weeks and left the builder to get on with it.

On his return, however, Luke found that the builder's work was not up to his standards. The floor didn't look right, the walls were supposed to be as smooth as glass, just like in five-star hotels. Loads of things were unsatisfactory and to make matters worse the builder couldn't even see where his work failed to meet Luke's standards.

The builder, whose most exotic holiday had been to Butlin's in Minehead, could not see the problem.

Luke brought the full force of his father's business legal department onto the builder and sued him, pursuing him relentlessly and tearing him apart financially.

The builder was powerless to defend himself against such financial might.

He was never paid for any of his work. He should have been allowed to put right whatever he could, but ultimately Luke should not have engaged someone to do a task that he was incapable of even envisaging, and then crush him.

This is bullying – a financial power trip.

We all love tales of when people take their power back from financial persecutors. John, a master joiner, had got a contract to install some windows for a local property developer who was well known for agreeing a price for a job without a written contract. Once the work was completed, knowing the tradesman would be desperate for the money, the developer's manager would come along, say the job was not good enough and offer half the agreed amount. He did this over and over again and it worked for him, because so many people come from a belief of *"I'm desperate so I have to accept this"*. John didn't.

The manager came to inspect the beautiful windows John had made and installed, then told the craftsman that all he would get was half the agreed price. John picked up his power saw, chopped the windows to bits and left.

The Creator

The only way to financial freedom is to learn how to create money. To do this you have to develop the *Rich* money mindset. Once you have learned and understood that, you never have to worry about money again.

Developing a *Rich* money mindset is done by learning how to add value, and then leveraging that value. It has never been easier to create money in any time in history than it is now. So much money has been created that the global wealth per person has risen exponentially over the last 100 years.

Look to yourself to find the solution to your problems. Learn, ask, seek out those who have achieved what you wish to, spend time with them, read their books, learn from them.

Be honest about where you are financially, because it is only from there that you can genuinely take the next step and improve.

Take complete responsibility for your own financial success. Stop taking responsibility for others. Financial support to help someone learn and grow is great; financial support that keeps somebody dis-empowered is nasty.

Through you adding value and creating new things others will gladly pay for, and more money is created. Think of the list of products and services that we buy now that didn't exist one hundred, fifty, or even 10 years ago. Human creativity and the pace of wealth creation is increasing exponentially.

What if Your Money Mindset is Rubbish?

What if you are not happy with your current money mindset? You can change your money mindset and choose one that gives you the results you want.

Many clients come to me because they are desperately unhappy with the financial results in their life, and are not living the lives they want because of financial problems. For example, I worked with a fabulous artist who was about to go back into full time employment and give up on her dream because she couldn't make her art support her. In a few sessions she changed her mindset from in-debt to rich and is now very successful. She learned to make the decisions of a rich person. She did not get a low-paying job, but leveraged her studio, time and skills to produce multiple income streams.

She now has a thriving studio and is curator of an art gallery. She is in business and making money from her art.

Another client wanted to run a business but knew she was paralysed by her fears. She was terrified of spending and wanted to keep working and build her business as well.

She shifted to understanding that this fear was exactly what was stopping her. She is now a wealthy and successful businesswoman.

I had to shift my own mindset from comfortable to rich. Because of my childhood traumas around money, I knew that my own mindset was stopping me from being successful and living the life I wanted.

Look at your current money mindset and ask yourself: is it serving me? Am I happy with the financial results in my life? Is what I have, what I want?

Discover Your Money Mindset

You can spot someone's money mindset from their bank statements. An individual with an in-debt mindset will show clearly that some of their income is being used to pay debt as soon as it hits the account. You might also see them borrowing money, so that the account begins to show a deficit towards the end of the month. Sometimes things get more serious and a great deal of the money coming into the account is immediately going to service debt. More debts are taken on with the minimum payments being made. In extreme cases people don't open their statements or bills.

Somebody with a *Break-even* mindset will show fixed expenses being covered first and then the rest being spent. Often when they get their bank statement or print it off, they have a quick glance and shove it in a drawer.

Somebody with a *Comfortable* mindset will show savings first, probably automated. They will open their statement, regularly check their bank balance, and file all statements. They will always live on less than they earn.

Someone with a *Rich* money mindset consistently monitors their accounts. You will see multiple bank accounts. All money will be used with intention, going to where it can work hard to make more money.

You will see the flow. The person with the rich mindset will regularly check the performance of all these accounts, making financial adjustments to ensure optimum wealth growth, and transferring money if needed. You will see savings used for the purpose of wealth growth, some for wealth protection but never just hoarded.

Your bank statements are the record and mirror of your financial decisions. Your decisions are at the heart of your money mindset. If you want to change your current mindset to another, start with your bank statements. First, look at where you are. It is much more effective if you can put together at least six months of your bank statements, then use these as a basis for the exercise. If you do not have your statements to hand, begin by looking at the exercise and entering your best guess.

Action Steps

Tracking your Money Behaviours

1. Get a record of your last six months financial transactions.

Bank statements are great for this. Include all your accounts and also stocks, bonds, annuities, premium bonds, even cheque/current and savings accounts. In other words, all of your financial records.

Get five highlighter pens.

- Use Colour 1 to highlight every time you have given money.
- Use Colour 2 to highlight every debt you pay.

For example, mortgage payment, car finance payment, bank loan, credit card bill, interest, overdraft.

- Use Colour 3 to show every time you spend money.

Rent, council tax, petrol and car tax, repairs; food; entertainment and so on. Every time you spend something and you pay for it out of available, not borrowed, funds; but include any spending on a credit card that you always clear every month. The total will be 'spent', i.e., cleared, at the end of the month.

- Use Colour 4 to highlight all of your savings.

Include here any financial products over which you do not have direct control. For example, a pension plan set up by an employer; or an 'investment plan' sold by a broker as a financial product or schemes that you allow a broker to run or a manager to make investment decisions on your behalf.

- Use Colour 5 to show all investments/assets you have personal control over that produce money for you.

For example, buying stocks and shares, business equipment, property, etc, everything you buy to get a financial return. Also show profits from leveraged money, e.g. income from rent, dividends, business profits, investments.

What do you see? What happens when money comes in? What is the first thing that happens? Is some automatically sucked out to cover debt? Does some go to pay debts? Do you pay your expenses first and live on what is left? Do you save first and live on what's left? Do you invest and leverage your funds?

1. Monthly income
2. How much came in from trading your time for money? (Job wages or self-employed?)
3. How many times did money come in from assets, i.e., investments/systematised businesses / properties
4. How many times did you give money?
5. How many personal debts do you pay?
6. How many times did you spend money?
7. How many times did you save money?
8. How many times did you leverage money?

This will give you some powerful pointers towards your mindset, and where you can start to make a change.

What are your results?

- Are you mostly paying off personal debts and are any personal debts left unpaid at the end of the week/month/quarter?

- Are you covering expenses and spending almost all you have with little left over for long term saving?
- Do you automatically save and live on the rest?
- Is every penny spent with intention?
- Does your cash flow from your assets, businesses and investments?

When you have looked at your bank statements and filled in the template, let's look at the pattern of your actions. What actions do you do most: give, borrow, spend, pay expenses first, save, leverage?

- Pay some debts.
- Give money to someone.
- Pay expenses.
- Save.
- Leverage.
- Sell time in exchange for money.
- Get money from assets.

Which money mindset do you have?

In-Debt	Break-Even	Comfortable	Rich
Borrow	Spend	Save	Leverage
Give	Give	Give	Give
Spend	Save	Spend	Spend

Chapter 7

Going Deeper
Our Words Reveal Our Money Mindset

The language we use is a pure reflection of what we believe, think and feel. When you really listen, you will find that people always tell the truth by what they say even if they don't realise it. Learn to listen well and you will be able tell a huge amount about someone's money mindset and their values and beliefs around money.

Consider the following everyday phrases. What mindset do you think that someone who makes these statements might have? Is the person spouting these clichés rich or poor? Do they have a below or above average income? Do they feel they have enough money or not? Do these people feel powerful or powerless with the money in their lives?

'Make hay while the sun shines'

Really saying: 'Grab short term opportunities while you can.'

Paying attention to someone saying this once saved us a fortune. In 2005 I was going to invest a substantial sum of money in another person's business.

As we talked he mentioned that his philosophy was to 'make hay while the sun shines'. I quickly shut down the meeting and had nothing more to do with him. Two months later he had gone bankrupt.

'I can't resist a bargain'

Really saying: 'I have to spend; and I have no impulse control and I cannot delay gratification.'

'Live for today'

Really saying: 'I don't delay gratification.'
And possibly reflects an *In-debt* mindset.

'Riches have wings'

Possible interpretation: 'Money can disappear easily.'
Money is like a bird with wings – it can fly away if you are not careful. What the speaker is actually saying is: 'I have an *In-debt* or *Break-even* mindset and no idea how to hold on to money.'

'Save for a rainy day'

Interpretation: 'It is prudent to save for bad times ahead.'
Really saying: 'I have a *Comfortable* money mindset and having big savings makes me feel secure.'

'Look after the pennies and the pounds will look after themselves'

Really saying: 'I'm good at managing money; I'm not so good at creating it.'
The speaker is coming from a place of fear and probably does not feel confident in their ability to create money.

'Money talks'

Interpretation: 'People with money have power and influence.'

Really saying: 'I believe people with money are more powerful.'

The speaker is making a judgment about people with money and the term may even be intended to be derogatory. It can also be a sign of someone believing they are a victim and powerless because they lack money.

'Time is money'

Interpretation: 'Don't waste time; treat it with as much respect as if it were money.'

Really saying: 'I don't understand the true value of time, which is infinitely more important than money.'

If I wasted a million pounds I could get it back; if I waste one hour I can never get that back. This statement gives money much more importance than it has.

'Opportunities are everywhere'

Really saying: 'I have a rich money mindset and I can always find an opportunity to make money. I know the means to create money are everywhere around me.'

'The early bird catches the worm'

Interpretation: 'You need to be there first to get the good stuff.'

Really saying: 'I have a comfortable money mindset; I believe opportunity is scarce. And you need to work very hard to earn money.'

'Less talk, more action'
Really saying: 'I have a *Rich* money mindset.'

'The Lord helps those who help themselves'
Really saying: 'You have to take personal responsibility for your financial success.'
May reflect a *Rich* or *Comfortable* mindset.

'Build a better mousetrap and the world will beat a path to your door'
Really saying: 'I have a *Rich* money mindset.'
Learn to add value and you will always be rich.

'Neither a borrower nor a lender be'
Really saying: 'I do not agree with debt, and have a *Break-even* mindset.'
The speaker does not understand the power of leveraging in building wealth.

'The rich get richer and the poor get poorer'
Really saying: 'I have very little power around my financial success.'
Probably comes from an individual with an *In-debt* or *Break-even* mindset.

'Rich people stay rich by living like they are broke; broke people stay broke by living like they are rich'
Shows awareness of the need to save money to ensure financial security, coming from a *Comfortable* money mindset.

'Money isn't everything'

Really saying: 'To me money isn't important.'

In essence, the speaker is saying that they are not willing to make the change to ensure they will have enough money in life.

'You have to have money to make money'

What do people really mean when they say this?

Think about it: literally, it means that you cannot make money without first having some. Just like you cannot make a beef steak without killing a cow. This is just not true! Of course you can make money without having any! For example, I found a fireplace in a skip and sold it – which meant I was able to make money without actually having any funds to invest.

If this saying was really true then there would be no money creation in the world because someone would have to have had funds before being able to generate more. Just because you don't have money doesn't mean you have no resources. People built wealth before money was invented. There was always a *Rich* money mindset: individuals who were able to look at the resources around them and figure out how they could be used to make more and better.

Time, knowledge and skills can be used to make money. People with a *Rich* money mindset know that resources are all around them; they just need to be able to recognise them to use them.

What people who recite this cliché really mean is that having to develop the knowledge and skills to make money is too much effort, like saying they have missed the goal without even trying to hit the ball, let alone put the hard work into becoming a great goal scorer. When you hear this saying, you are hearing an excuse.

It is like stating that 'because I'm not successful, I can't become successful' or 'because I'm not rich, I can't become rich.' Anyone who has gone from nothing to success or wealth (and there are plenty of people who have) is proof that with the right mindset, anyone can do it. When you know how money really works, you will be able to find the resources to make money.

'If you pay peanuts you get monkeys'

This is certainly not true. So many great people work for very little money. They just don't ask for what they want or deserve.

Frightened people work for peanuts.

I knew a computer programmer in his 50s who had been made redundant and suffered a terrible knock to his self-esteem. He walked with his head down and exuded dejection and failure.

As a result, an unscrupulous businessman took advantage of his situation by employing him on a shameful pittance, a rate that he has continued to pay to this day. This employer has built his business model around being able to employ people who are at an all-time low and whose confidence has been crushed. None of his employees are stupid, and they are certainly not monkeys. They are fearful of being sacked if they ask for what they are worth.

'Money doesn't grow on trees'

This hackneyed saying is rubbish! What it really means is: 'I do not have enough money; it's not freely available; the supply is finite; you can't just plant more trees to get more.'

This money mindset is one that does not understand the power of leverage.

'You need a good qualification to fall back on'

We've all heard this popular wisdom: get a good qualification to fall back on – so if your dream doesn't work out, you have a backup for making a living. This is said by someone who expects failure. It is untrue.

Do you think that any rich person, who spent years learning to build businesses and create wealth, thinks, 'If this doesn't work out I'll get a job with my university qualification?' Of course they don't.

If all went wrong, someone with a *Rich* money mindset would use their experience of creating wealth to do it again.

I love the story of Bruce Springsteen's mother who said of her famous musician son, "He should finish college so that he has something to fall back on if the music thing doesn't work out".

Now you know what you are telling yourself in the clichés that you use, what sayings will you no longer use?

What Do You Believe about Money?

The best way to identify your beliefs around money is to examine your financial results. Do your results come from beliefs that have been passed on to you by others or from previous experiences that are no longer relevant? Track them back. From every result, work back to:

- the action that caused the result
- the decision that led to the action
- the thought that led you to make that decision
- the feelings that led to the thoughts
- the values you hold that make that decision important
- the beliefs that underlie the values

Try the exercise on the next page.

Results	Actions	Decisions	Thoughts	Feelings	Values	Beliefs
Debt						
Savings						
Investments						
Financial Losses						
Financial Gains						
Working at something I don't like for money						

Bigger, Better, Faster, Longer

Go to school, study hard; go to university, study hard; get a career, work harder and harder. Miss out on time with your family. Even choose not to have a family so it doesn't interfere with your career. Along the way buy stuff to show how successful you are: big car, big holidays, big house (because after all, your big house is an asset).

I did this. When I was growing up I saw how terrible my parents' lives became because they hated their jobs. My aunt hated her job even more. I wanted to do something different, so set up a chimney-sweeping business when I left university and loved it! My parents went mad, and could not stand the disgrace of a daughter covered in soot, living in a small house in a poor area while building her business.

I then did the most stupid thing of my life. I conformed. I allowed the negative feedback and hostility to break me down.

My 23 year old ego couldn't cope with being regarded as doing something degrading, and with people judging me as inferior. It touched my Catholic shame button and rather than having the vision, self-belief and courage to be myself, and grow and nurture my business-building skills, I chickened out.

I went to London, joined the corporate rat race, married an investment banker and lived a thoroughly joyless working life until I found the guts to leave and set up in business again at 40. I lost so much by conforming – in total about 18 years of my life. No amount of money on earth, even Bill Gates' fortune 10 times over, can buy back a single day of those 18 years.

If you learn how to create wealth rather than earn money, you will be so much more secure.

People are encouraged to give up their lives in exchange for the trappings of success. When I was a debt adviser, I saw many people with executive homes and impressive cars who described lying awake at night, terrified about how they could continue to keep up with financing these extravagances.

I could see the pain of these people struggling with huge financial commitments to create an illusion of wealth for others. Every time they got a promotion, they got a bigger house or car to reflect how they were becoming more successful. I had seen from my rich relatives and the rich people I interviewed that the trappings of wealth came after building businesses and after investments had produced the wealth to support them. They never bought the trappings from debt that depended on a job for payment.

Many people believe that their home and car are assets. Your home is not an asset. It costs you money to finance, and even if you have paid your mortgage, try not paying your bills for a while and see how financially free you are.

A home is also a liability in another way. People get tied into their homes emotionally and continue to do jobs they hate to keep it. It's bad enough to keep doing something because you resist change and fear upsetting people, but to give your time, life and energy to maintaining a house! I have done this in the past and know that it is so sad.

I have seen people defer living because they needed others to see how successful they were by the stuff they owned. Think about that seriously. Are you going to devote your life to showing others (probably those who have hurt you) how materially successful you are? Or are you just going to live your life doing what you value and believe in?

Such trappings are distractions from living the life you could be living. Once you build true wealth from assets, you can have all the trappings you choose.

'Save for a pension/get a good job with a pension'

This advice is the biggest lie of all.

The government is continually giving us the message that we are not saving enough for our old age. When they say this, they are referring to people who do not work for the government. State employees in the UK receive massive state-funded pensions in comparison to people who work in the private sector.

Those of us who are non-state employees fret over how to provide for ourselves in old age, feeling frightened, guilty and overwhelmed. We know we should do something but are not sure exactly what to do. We are not convinced that saving or paying into a pension, as we have been advised, is the right thing to do. We know it is hugely expensive and we really don't know if we will get anything back. There are many examples of people who have contributed to a pension in good faith, only to receive next to nothing when they retire. No wonder so few of us have made the pension provision we are supposed to. Deep down, we feel our money is disappearing into some sort of black hole. The fees for arranging a pension, which the majority of us do not understand, mean that someone else ends up with the financial security; the fees may look low, but end up high. Pension companies and brokers get richer while the pension holder gets very little back. Tony Robbins, author and motivational speaker, in his book *Money* shows how this works.

What you believe and end up doing about pensions and retirement is a direct reflection of your money mindset.

Those with a *Rich* money mindset believe that because they can create money, they can choose when and how they retire. Many with this mindset never retire because they enjoy the process and challenge of creating money so much they never stop.

Those with a *Comfortable* money mindset might take deferred gratification to its ultimate tragic end. We have all heard stories of people who retired on full pension after 40 years' hard slog, only to drop dead within weeks.

Saving and deferred gratification are invaluable when working towards building wealth however when it comes to retirement and pensions you need to understand that no matter how careful you are, old age is not going to end well. Death is inevitable.

To spend your whole life deferring gratification, doing something unfulfilling in order to stay in a pension scheme and have an income for those last few years of your life is futile. Surely it is better to learn how to invest in low charge tracker funds or other investments ourselves and control when we want to start living a little.

"Don't spend 40 years building someone else's dream, so that you can have a few years at the end to build yours."

I am not saying that we should abandon plans to provide for ourselves in the future. I am saying we need to develop the financial skills to provide for ourselves now, so that we can live the life we want today, rather than waiting for some imaginary time in the future.

People with a *Break-Even* money mindset contribute to a pension and then live modestly within their means on the pension allowance.

They end their days much the same way as they started, by breaking even.

Those with an *In-Debt* money mindset try to avoid thinking about retirement at all until the time comes, then find ways to raise money to spend by, for example, releasing equity from their houses, taking out loans, selling their belongings and other desperate schemes.

'Loads of savings are a good thing'

We have been trained to think that saving for a rainy day is a good thing. To have an allotted sum set aside to deal with an emergency is vital because otherwise even a small emergency can become a financial disaster. However, beyond that, continuing to hoard money in savings displays low financial intelligence. Hoarding money stops us from doing good with it. Money should be used as a tool not a security blanket. The risk is that if you constantly save for a rainy day, you'll end up with a storm.

Geraldine was an extreme example of this. She had been taught by her mother from a young age to always save for a rainy day. She inherited a huge sum of money from her at 21, and could have purchased 10 houses in any high end global city. Instead, she purchased a modest house and banked the rest. For the next 50 years, she eked out the money in the bank, spending it sparingly to make it last as long as possible.

She saved on house repairs and heating and put up with water streaming through the roof and down the walls every time it rained. Ironically, she lived through the 'rainy day' most of her life.

When she had been living frugally for nearly 30 years a wealthy friend offered to repair her house and she flatly refused, preferring to live as she did with her house falling to pieces around her. She felt safe and secure and in control living on very little.

My father, suffered a similar plight sitting on a fortune in shares while living in penury and detesting his job. He pressured my mother into working a further two years in her 60s despite ill-health.

These examples show that many are afraid of making money and creating wealth. We are taught to borrow or hoard, but never to make money work for us. We don't understand this concept and so give money power over us that it should not have.

I always had a big pot of savings that I called my 'F**k You money', because it meant I always had enough to be able to walk away from any job if I wanted to. It was only as I got older that I understood I had the power to say 'F**k You' all along. I did not need a stash of money to feel OK about walking away and doing my own thing.

Choosing Different Beliefs

Everything that you need is available to you if you could only see that! You only have to choose to believe it. Your biggest challenge is to change the beliefs that are holding you where you are and giving you unwanted results. What if you believed you are successful? What sort of decisions would you make every day if you came from a belief of being a successful person? The truth is, nothing will happen to make you successful; you have to believe that you are, or that you will be, and then think, feel and act that way to generate successful results in your life.

If you changed your beliefs, you would change your decisions and actions and the results would be change in your life. The most important step is to take responsibility.

You are responsible for your beliefs and you are responsible for choosing new beliefs if your current beliefs don't serve you.

*"It's our choices that show who we truly are,
far more than our abilities."*
JK Rowling, Acclaimed multi-millionaire author

The Emotional Connection

Money beliefs and values come from the incidents, good and bad, that happened in childhood. We attached meaning to key financial events in our youth and unless we become aware of those events, and challenge and change the associated meanings, we are destined to play them out again and again throughout our lives.

You can get a good idea of the meaning of financial incidents in your past by exploring your financial timeline.

Exercise

Your Money Timeline

1. Take a sheet of paper and begin at the far left side of the page. Think of your earliest memory of money.

As you think back to that first memory of money, become aware of what you are seeing: who was there? What were they doing? What was happening? What were you hearing? What were they saying? How were they saying it? At that time, what were you feeling? And what were the people around you feeling? What meaning did you give to money at that instant?

If it was a positive or happy memory, put a number from 0 to 5 to indicate that above the line.

The greater the happiness, the higher from the timeline your number would be. If it was a negative or painful memory write a number from 0 to -5, depending on the intensity of the feeling. If it was a neutral memory write your score on the timeline.

Continue along your timeline up to the present day, writing down your most memorable money experiences – as many as you can. These money experiences may not be something that someone else would regard as important. That is not the issue. What matters is that they were important to you at the time.

Remember that experiences of poverty and wealth are extremely individual and comparative. Don't dismiss an event that had a major effect on you because somebody else might believe it's not important or that it shouldn't have mattered. If it caused you discomfort or happiness, it did matter. Recognise and record as many of these instances as you can.

2. Once you have reached the present, go back to each incident and identify a few words that describe how you felt at each moment: e.g. disappointed, angry, betrayed, controlled, favoured, unfulfilled, safe, secure, sad, embarrassed, fearful, happy, excited, shameful, etc. If you can't remember, imagine how you would have felt or how someone else might have felt.

3. Look at all the feelings, and use one or two sentences to encapsulate the beliefs about money you have formed. The sequence of events is important because it will help you understand how you built assumptions on top of others, and how a young mind intensifies events.

4. Complete the following sentence:

My life's experience of money has given me [write in here the appropriate words as they come to mind] .... money beliefs.

You now have a clearer picture of your mindset around money.

One lady who did this exercise could clearly see her underlying belief that big savings keep you safe and give you control. Fiona is in her 50s. She described her terror when her father's business collapsed when she was seven years old. For a year, her father stuck his head in the sand and lost everything. Fiona vividly painted a picture of electricity being disconnected and the bank threatening to take the house. For her, not spending meant she would never have to rely on anyone else.

The key here is awareness. Once you can identify the emotions that formed your money mindset, you can understand that they made perfect sense at that time.

Fiona, at the age of seven, felt completely out of control and powerless to do anything constructive to prevent the financial situation from getting any worse, so as an adult she decided to hoard money in a bid to feel safe and in control.

However, this action damaged her ability to generate wealth because she was afraid to make financial decisions that would grow the business instead of playing it safe and not growing.

Of course, if you identify emotions and beliefs that are not serving you and you choose to change them, remember that those around you with the same beliefs will almost definitely not change theirs.

This is one of the consequences of growth. Sometimes, the people around you will not come with you.

Don't Feel Bad or Ashamed …

I have coached many people on how to understand and change their money mindset. People often beat themselves up about bad decisions they have made with money. Avoid beating yourself up about the actions you took because of an old money mindset.

This is what you had learned in your life and at the time you were doing the best you could. Most of us at some point make poor money decisions, don't understand how to make better ones and suffer shame and powerlessness.

How can you learn about financial success in a world where people won't talk about money? In a world where they would prefer to give you details of their sex life rather than their financial life? People all over the world lie about money, pretending they have either more or less than they really do, depending on what emotional issues they have around the subject. Money is intrinsically connected with our self-worth and the value society puts on us.

At various times in our lives, young or old, we feel 'not good enough'. Everyone feels it in some way.

Big corporations understand and exploit this 'not good enough' belief and feeling. Everywhere around us we get messages that if we buy this or that product we will be more desirable. Corporate advertising exploits our children, peddling expensive consumer goods and instilling the idea that owning these products will make them of more value as a person.

In schools, children who do not have designer clothes and the latest tech can be mercilessly bullied. Nearly every parent will cave in when a crying child explains why he/she feels left out because he/she doesn't have the latest. Even if a parent has to go into debt, they will usually buy the item to appease their child. I often hear parents say they will do anything so their child can have what they didn't have. The problem here is that the parent is not learning to deal with the link between self-worth and material goods; it is not about making sure, no matter what, that the child always has everything they desire. Some parents feel guilty if their child has to deal with the normal rigours of life. This type of deep parental guilt is normal: we all experience it, but to be financially successful and to teach our children how to be financially successful, getting into debt to buy consumer goods is not the right answer.

Reclaiming our power around the money and self-worth is essential. Our value is never commensurate with the amount of money we have in our bank accounts or the car we drive.

An *In-debt* money mindset will make us feel inferior, inadequate and excluded. An *In-debt* money mindset is driven by these beliefs is common and preyed upon. Fight it and beat it, but don't feel shame at having been there. Shame keeps us trapped in old mindsets.

You *Can* Change Your Money Mindset

In my work I have helped many people change their money mindset. You too can change your money mindset if you are prepared to put in the deep level work that such change demands.

Myrna was a young mother with three children. She had little formal education and since having her children had lived on welfare. She was permanently mired in debt, and it eventually got so deep that she was being harassed by debt collectors. She would hide in bed wondering whether today would be the day the bailiffs would come and take everything she owned or even evict her.

Myrna ran an *In-debt* mindset. When we explored what she wanted, she felt that to get to a *Rich* or even *Comfortable* mindset was too big a stretch. The result she wanted was to get out, and stay out, of debt.

Step by step we agreed a plan with goals and milestones. Then we began to explore what might derail the plan. She identified shopping in a superstore. She felt a compulsion to fill the trolley high.

Digging a little deeper she suddenly said: "It's clear now."

She could see herself sitting in a trolley as a very young child with her 'happy mum'.

"When I was a child, my mother would pile the super-market trolley high when she was happy, and sing as we went around the supermarket. Then my father lost his job and we had no money so the pile in the trolley was low. My mother would angrily say: "Only small trolleys from now on, because your father is not working." I sat in the trolley looking at my sad angry mum, and associated the feeling with the low trolley."

As a grown woman and mother herself, as soon as she had any money, Myrna would recreate this happy mum feeling by piling the supermarket trolley high. Once Myrna made the link, we developed a plan to change her *In-debt* money mindset and she has never been in debt since.

Robin, a very successful businessman, came to me for coaching. He was turning over £20,000 a week, but was haemorrhaging money. On our first session, bankruptcy was only a few steps away.

The *4 Money Mindsets* logo was visible in my office, and I noticed that when he saw 'debt' written down, he turned away from the disturbing word and sat almost in a curled-up foetal position, so intense was his distress. I could feel his pain. We looked at his plan and goals for getting his business and his wellbeing back on an even keel.

He sat in the chair, rocking back and forth, saying to himself: "What an idiot, what an idiot."

We investigated a little deeper. His father had been a coal miner. When the pits were closed, the people were left with nothing and his family was desperately poor.

Robin did not want to be like the villagers from the area where he grew up so he worked hard to build a successful business. He did fabulously well and should have been the happiest man on earth.

However, the more money that came into the business, the more he was able to borrow: he had a Porsche, a Maserati, a mansion, racehorses, sent his children to the best private schools, and had countless other trappings of financial success.

As soon as he understood his pattern we created a plan for change. He was an amazing man and his mindset shifted immediately. He put our plan in place and turned things around from that moment. Today he still has a large house and sends his kids to even better schools, because that is what he values. He has 'only' one car and no longer has any horses, because he has stopped feeling that his possessions reflect his value as a person.

Whatever money mindset you have and whatever situation you are in, you can change your beliefs and your life at this very instant.

Change? Or stay comfortable?

Deep level change is not for everybody. To change your money mindset you will have to change your behaviour. This is going to be uncomfortable at best; excruciatingly painful at worst. However, if you persist you will succeed. There is no easy way round this – make the change or stay the same. Nobody, but nobody, can do it for you.

The world is full of people who have been conned by 'get rich quick' schemes. A get rich quick scheme offers big returns for a relatively small investment with the founder of the scheme supposedly putting in all the hard work. If that were really the case wouldn't the founder of the scheme raise the small financial input themselves and reap the rewards for themselves?

Nobody can do the sit ups for you if you want to have a six-pack.

Nothing Grows in the Comfort Zone

When I coach people I teach them how to change their mindset step by step. We work one step at a time through how they developed their money mindset, and what specifically they need to do to reach their financial destination. I can guide and throw light on what holds them back and what they need to do, but it is the client who does the hard work.

Getting out of your comfort zone and refusing to slip back into bad habits takes courage, and a willingness to take the first tentative steps when you don't know what's next, because your direction and goals in life are so unfamiliar and different. Many find this just too uncomfortable.

We all have the choice. A lady I know, who is very well-educated with a good job, complains but never initiates big change in her life. She says, "People don't have choices because sometimes these choices are too hard." What she is really saying is that making significant changes in her life is, for her, too difficult. So she doesn't, and continues to complain.

Think about your own comfort zones and habits. Do you have a habit of overspending? Do you respect the money you have – or not? Do you have a habit of hoarding? Do you regularly feel/say that you can't afford something? Are these comfort zones that you need to grow out of?

Why Most People Don't Change

Most people prefer to stay in their comfort zone and complain about the life they live. They find it too hard to change or are scared to make the necessary changes.

To change your money mindset, you must develop tremendous courage and tenacity. You will reap great rewards, but will also have to let go of comfortable habits that are a key part of your current identity. You will have to change what you believe, what you do, and possibly some friends or accept a changed relationship with some family members. People are often very resistant when those close to them choose to fundamentally change.

The only way to change what you habitually do is to change your mindset. If you want to be rich, you must do what rich people do on a daily basis. Make the decisions and take the actions that rich people do. Learn about business and finances. Be prepared to do what it takes. Use your money and your time the way a rich person does, and you will end up rich.

If you want to stay as you are, that is OK. You can achieve this by continuing to do what you have been doing.

To succeed in changing your money mindset, however, you need to get comfortable with being uncomfortable. In other words, you have to acknowledge you will feel uncomfortable in order to change and grow. Every time you are out of your comfort zone in terms of your money mindset, know that you are growing and feel good about it. Learn to relish the uncertainty and the struggle, all of which shows you are successful and have the courage to be who and what you want to be.

Action Steps

Recognising Your Own and Others' Money Mindsets

- Recognise your own money mindset.
- Learn to recognise the money mindset of the people around you.
- Identify your limiting beliefs around money.

Part 4

Shifting Your Money Mindset

Chapter 8

Shifting Your Money Mindset
Step-by-Step

In this chapter we will explore each of the specific steps you need to take to shift your money mindset. We will look first at the general steps required for any mindset shift, from smoker to non-smoker, unhealthy to healthy, procrastinator to action-oriented, etc. Then we will look at the precise steps needed for money mindset change.

Where Do You Want to Get to?

There is an old saying: "If I had known I wanted to get over there, I wouldn't have started from here."

However, you are (as they say) where you are. The problem for most people is that they don't know where they are. The key to understanding this is to know your own money mindset, which will give you a totally honest appraisal of where you are.

The next important step is to decide exactly where you want to get to and which money mindset you want. Most people don't understand that the choice is theirs to take. Most people don't end up rich or different from their parents and peers because they never think it's possible. They are just running the mindsets of the people closest to them without even realising it.

Imagine your goal in detail. Build a vivid, mental picture using all your senses – notice in that picture what is around you, what you can see, hear and feel. Then, when you have a clear vision of the mindset you want, commit to your decision and be willing to pay the price to achieve it.

In reality, few are willing to pay that price.

I once had a prospective client who was adamant that she was miserable with her financial situation and would do anything to change it. When I outlined the steps she would need to take for mindset change, she left and never came back. Two years later she was still in the same job, the same financial position and the same state of misery.

In most cases, a person is not willing to make the tough choices necessary to get what they want in life. The only person who reaps the rewards is the one who faces and makes tough decisions.

Being prepared to make such decisions will involve changing your mindset. To do that …

1. Identify where you are now. This is critical.
2. Identify what you want.
3. Be very specific – build a clear, vivid mental image.
4. Be very clear about why you want it.
5. Decide to take action – and fully commit to doing what is necessary to achieve your goal.
6. Accept/understand that this means a whole new way of life. Restructure your life to support your decision.
7. Take the actions you need to support your new life. For example, move house, associate with the people you want to emulate, who are already living the type of life you want to create for yourself.

It is only by working through these steps that you develop clarity. With that clarity comes the realisation of how big a shift some mindset changes will lead to. You don't become successful because something amazing happens in your life; something amazing happens in your life because you are taking the steps to be successful every day.

In the same way, your life doesn't generally change because something amazing happens from outside, but if you actively change your life, you are clearing the path for something amazing to happen easily.

To change your mindset you must change your beliefs, values, feelings, thoughts, decisions and actions. Then the new results will definitely show up. You have to commit to becoming the sort of person who gets those results in their life.

While it's entirely possible to go from an *In-Debt* mindset to a *Rich* one – and I've had clients achieve this – it is much more common for people to choose to move up the mindsets one by one, for example from *In-Debt* to *Break-Even*, *Break-even* to *Comfortable* or *Comfortable* to *Rich*.

Often clients choose to change one little step at a time, which is an effective way of bringing about big changes in your financial life. It is important to understand that taking small positive steps consistently will eventually lead to transformation. A little step every day to challenge your money mindset and choose new beliefs will soon produce new beliefs, values, feelings, thoughts, decisions, actions and ultimately real results.

From In-Debt to Break-Even

You are committing to become a different person around money. You are committing to deep change. To change from an in-debt money mindset to a break-even money mindset:

1. Identify where you are now. This is critical.

If you are in debt, you must understand and accept the exact specifics of how much money is owed, to whom, etc.

2. Identify what you want.

Which new mindset do you want? What results do you want? For example, do you want to avoid ever being in debt again, have no concerns about savings, take control of finances for the future, or run a business and become wealthy? Many of my clients just want to break even. Whatever you want is right for you.

3. Be very clear about why you want it.

If you are not 100% clear about your goals you will find it very hard to continually motivate yourself. If you are doing it for the wrong reason and not totally aligned, then your efforts won't work. Be clear and completely honest with yourself.

4. Fully commit to doing what is necessary to achieve your goal.

If you want to get out and stay out of debt forever, then fully committing to that is essential.

5. Accept that this means a whole new way of life.

From now on, you will become a person who never gets into debt, who always lives within their means.

People used to you being the sort of person who gets into debt may not be happy with this change in you. Think of your relationships with other adults or children: will you be shifting your money mindset while someone with whom you have joint financial responsibility is not? There will be things and people you will need to let go of. Your life will be different. Accept it.

6. Restructure your life to support your decision.

You will need to make big changes. Like an alcoholic shifting their mindset, may mean doing different things – for entertainment, eating differently, shopping differently, making different plans ... and so on.

7. Take the actions you need to support your new life.

Do what you need to do to create a new life. Associate only with the people want to emulate, who are already living the type of life you want to create for yourself.

Changing your current beliefs from ones that keep you in debt to ones that enable you to break even.

The following are the new beliefs, values, feelings, thoughts, decisions and actions that you must adopt as habits to guarantee the break-even results.

The Break-Even Money Mindset

Beliefs

- I am becoming someone who manages money very well.
- I am organised, diligent and responsible.
- I am good at managing money.

Values

- Being responsible with money.
- People who manage their money are good, diligent, organised and responsible.

Feelings

- I feel good about myself because things are on target due to the work I am doing.
- When my plan deviates from target, I feel uncomfortable. I need to get things back on target.
- I feel confident in my ability to manage money on a pay-cheque-to-pay-cheque basis.

Thoughts

- What do I need to do today to manage my money effectively?
- How do I make my money stretch further?

Decisions

- I make all my decisions based on whether I am sticking to my financial targets.

Actions

- I act on my decisions quickly and readily.

Results

- I always pay my bills on time and my day-to-day finances are always in order. Often things I want are not in the budget but I deal with this easily and plan for them in the future if they are true necessities. I always break even or have a little left over. I am never in debt.

From Break-Even to Comfortable

You are committing to become a different person around money. To change from a break-even money mindset to a comfortable money mindset is a big shift. You are committing to saving and creating a large surplus of money in your life:

1. Identify where you are now. This is critical.

You must analyse and thoroughly understand the detail of your current finances. You must understand exactly how much is coming in, and exactly how much is going out and to whom.

2. Identify what you want.

You need to understand what you really want. For example, do you want to amass large savings, maybe build provision for your later life? Do you want to feel secure by way of being capable of providing your own financial security through taking responsibility for your finances?

3. Be very clear about why you want it.

If you are not 100% clear about this you will find it very hard to continually motivate yourself. Be crystal clear that this is the financial result you want. To achieve this shift you will have to make some pretty tough choices. Do you want the change enough to be OK with this?

4. Decide to take action and fully commit to doing what is necessary to achieve the new mindset.

If you want to amass large savings and feel financially secure, then fully committing to this goal is essential.

5. Accept that this means a whole new way of life.

From now on whenever you get any money, you will save a portion of it first. You will do this regardless of what other expenses you need to cover. You will not spend your savings, no matter what. Needing to break into them for an emergency is not an option. You will find another way to deal with the emergency. People used to you being the person who spends all their money freely and readily dips into any surplus may not be happy with this change in you. Think of your relationships with other adults and children: will you be shifting your money mindset while someone with whom you have joint financial responsibility is not? There will be things and people that you will need to let go of. Your life will be different. Accept it.

6. Restructure your life to support your decision.

You will need to make big changes in your life. Like a drug addict shifting their mindset you will have to structure your life to reflect your new mindset. You will be doing everyday things very differently – shopping differently, maybe in different places, doing different things for entertainment, eating differently, holidaying differently …

7. Take the actions you need to support your new life.

For example, associate with the people that you want to emulate who are already living the type of life you want to create for yourself.

Supporting this mindset change means changing your current beliefs from those that keep you breaking even to those that make you comfortable.

The following are the new beliefs, values, feelings, thoughts, decisions and actions you must adopt as habits to guarantee comfortable results.

The Comfortable Money Mindset

Beliefs

- I am completely responsible for my financial security.
- I am a diligent and responsible person.
- I am financially strategic, organised and systematic.
- It is imperative to have savings; it is possible to amass great savings, regardless of my income level.
- I must always save for a rainy day.
- My big savings give me security.
- I only take financial risks with money I can afford to lose.
- People who save before they spend are virtuous and responsible.
- People have no need of most items, especially not if it gets them into debt.

Values

- Planning for the future.
- Delaying gratification.
- Excellent at managing and extremely responsible with money.
- Saving assiduously.
- Being aware of the many financial risks and taking appropriate actions and precautions.

Feelings

- Interest rates are going up and because I have no consumer debt I feel comfortable and safe.
- I look at those who have taken out big loans to live the high life and would not like to be in their position.
- I want to feel secure and protected by my financial position.
- I feel frightened when something threatens my financial security.

Thoughts

- I must ensure I am financially secure.
- I must keep up with what is happening out in the financial world so I can ensure my financial security.
- I anticipate changes in the external environment that might threaten my financial security.

Decisions

- I will always save a proportion of my income first before spending a single penny. Only then will I buy what I need.
- I do not take risks with my savings.

Actions

- I analyse and seek patterns in multiple sources of data to ensure my finances are secure.
- I create separate accounts:
- *A savings account:* I will automate a significant percentage of my income to go into this immediately after my salary is paid.
- *A bills account:* all my bills will be paid from this account.
- *A spending account:* I can spend what is left over in this account.

Results

- I keep my money.
- I have big savings.
- I always pay my bills on time.
- Because I am so money savvy and careful, I am eligible for all the best deals on phones, mortgages, etc.

From Comfortable to Rich

You are committing to become a totally different person around money. In changing from a comfortable to a rich money mindset you are committing to going from someone who earns money to someone who creates money. You will shift from someone who works for money to someone who gets money to work for you.

1. Identify where you are now. This is critical.

Be clear where you are. With a *Comfortable* money mindset you are hugely security conscious and risk averse. You have money locked up in savings or low risk investments that are not working very hard for you and giving you very little return.

2. Identify what you want.

3. Be very clear on why you want it.

Do you really want to be rich and become the sort of person who gains wealth? What is important to you about living the life of someone who is rich, and doing what it takes to be rich?

4. Decide to take action and fully commit to doing what is necessary to achieve this goal.

If this is genuinely what you want, completely commit to going for it. This will mean that you deeply challenge your insecurities and fears around money.

5. Accept that this means a whole new way of life.

Be willing to pay the price. Accept all that comes from making such a decision for your new life. You will have to step far out of your comfort zone and take risks in terms of doing things you have never done before, and really don't yet know how to do.

6. Restructure your life to support your decision.

Do everything you need to do to align with your new way of living. Be prepared to learn a whole new way of being and let go of the old way of being.

7. Take the actions you need to support your new life.

For example, move house, associate with the people that you want to emulate, who are already living the type of life you want to create for yourself. Read new books, learn new skills.

Supporting this mindset change means changing your current beliefs from those that keep you comfortable to those that make you rich.

These are the new beliefs, values, thoughts, feelings, decisions and actions you must adopt as habits to guarantee the rich results.

The Rich Money Mindset

Beliefs

- I am a rich person.
- I can create the amount of money I want in my life.
- Rich people create money from their minds; poor people work for money.
- Everyone has the opportunity to create wealth. Some take it and others choose not to. I believe and have faith that it can be done.
- I don't waste time, and I grab my chances.
- I know that we all have the same amount of time in each day. True wealth is generated from knowing how to use time.

Values

- Freedom to create wealth.
- Taking action to make a change for the better instead of complaining and feeling sorry for myself.
- Having the freedom to create my own life.
- Being able to choose the life I want.
- Creating wealth by adding value instead of selling my time.
- My time above all else.
- Making every second count.
- Having goals.
- Working hard.
- Tenaciously pursuing my goals and desires.

Feelings

- I have the urge to build and create.
- I feel the financial flow.
- I love the freedom of being in charge of my own life.
- I want to change.
- I want to try something new and exciting.
- I love learning.
- To be out of my comfort zone means I am getting better and improving my life.
- I feel tremendous fear, and recognise this as a sign of being out of my comfort zone and that I am growing.
- I am learning to enjoy the struggle.

Thoughts

- If something frightens me I will figure how to overcome it.
- Where is the next opportunity to create wealth?
- How would this or that business model work?
- I am continually searching. I am continually driven.
- How can I use resources to create more value?
- I focus on leveraging and creating value.
- When I fail, I will learn from it and keep going again and again.

Decisions

- I invest time in something that produces a return.
- I invest money to add value.
- I set goals. I plan. I prepare well.
- I make every penny count.
- I build my own assets and wealth

Actions

- I work on tasks that add value for a pre-planned number of hours every day.
- I work on the right stuff.
- I delegate well to the right people.
- I work hard.
- I take calculated risks.
- I work outside of my comfort zone.

Results

- I have financial freedom.
- I have assets that provide me with money.
- I am able to live my life as I choose.
- I am wealthy.
- I live my life on my own terms.

You Can Choose Your Money Mindset

You can choose any money mindset you want. I have explained how you can move from *In-Debt* to *Break-Even*, from *Break-Even* to *Comfortable* and from *Comfortable* to *Rich*. You can choose to move from any one to any other simply by following the steps for mindset change. You could choose to go from in-debt to rich or even from rich to in-debt, though I would question why anyone would want to do that!

By following the steps you will see the results. It works the same way as following the steps that someone with a slim mindset takes – you would end up slim if you continued to take those same steps. Someone who is slim focuses on staying slim. Someone who is in debt, breaks even, is comfortable or rich focuses on staying that way.

What are you focussing on?

Setting Your Money Mindset Goal

The important thing here is to set a goal that genuinely achieves change. Change that will show up in your finances: if your finances stay the same then you have not changed your money mindset. Change is achieved by following properly the seven steps to mindset change. Here's a case study.

1. Identify where you are now.

You might find this tough, which is natural. Many clients have said the most shocking insight they uncovered was their actual money mindset.

Vincent struggled with this. He initially stated that he had a number of accounts into which he automatically saved funds each month. At this point, his goal was to develop a rich money mindset and 'feel rich'.

As we worked, he revealed that he was up to his overdraft limit and needed a loan to meet his immediate financial commitments. A month later he failed to make contracted payments to a creditor, and the same thing happened the following month. He was again up to his (very large) overdraft limit and couldn't make due payments.

He was distressed by his circumstances and felt it was not representative of his usual financial behaviour.

When we explored further, however, examining the last 12 months' financial records, it was evident he had been up to his overdraft limit on many occasions.

Vincent was running an *In-debt* money mindset and found this excruciatingly painful to acknowledge. I felt such compassion for him because so many of us suffer shame and vicious self-deprecation when we haven't handled our money the way we wanted.

Vincent really struggled with this revelation and the biggest step for him in solving his money problems was to accept where he was and to be able to look at the situation in detail – not only at the figures, but also the emotions that had caused him to run the *In-debt* money mindset.

For myself, some years ago I found it difficult to accept I was running a *Comfortable* money mindset, and that it was seriously hampering my goal of financial freedom.

You may find this step difficult but the rewards are great if you can stick with it, go through your financial records and pin down your money mindset.

So, if you find this step difficult, go easy on yourself and take the time to understand where you are and to be OK with it.

2. Identify what you want in detail.

This is very important. Identify what you want in very specific detail. If it is too big a shift, you won't be able to visualise and create the detail you need to be able to make that shift. Remember, baby steps will eventually get you to the top of Everest as long as they are in the right direction. All you have to do is take the next step and the next and keep doing that until you have different financial results.

Vincent first had to develop a *Break-Even* money mindset. Through working together, he learned that he had to stop relying on borrowing to meet his day-to-day running costs. He had to learn to manage the money he had rather than thinking that getting more money would somehow solve his problems. He discovered the opposite was true: that when someone with an *In-Debt Money Mindset* gets more money they tend to get into even more debt – it makes the situation worse unless they change their mindset! Vincent identified that what he wanted was to always be able to meet all of his financial commitments on time, never fall into debt, and to become good at managing his money.

3. Why do you want it, exactly?

You must make sure you want this change for the right reasons. Doing it to please someone else or impress people is probably not a good enough reason. To shift your mindset requires hard work and personal challenges. You must want it on a deep level to keep motivated. Remember to write down your reason down and review your goal often to keep you going!

Vincent did not feel he could go through the discomfort and shame of failing to meet his financial commitments, and that had led to the borrowing habit. Every month he was in the same situation, and he now felt stressed and tired. He had done this for years and finally had enough. He admitted, "I can't bear to go on like this."

Remember to ask yourself why exactly you want this mindset change, write down every detail of your reason and review it often.

4. Decide to do it and fully commit to the decision.

Once you commit you must follow through. There is no halfway solution.

This was hard for Vincent. He committed to managing his finances without relying on borrowing. This meant he had to make different spending decisions and stick to them no matter what.

What will you decide and fully commit to follow through?

5. Accept that this means a whole new way of life.

For Vincent this meant becoming a person who never got into debt. If he did not have enough money to buy something he wanted, he did without or saved up. It also meant telling his adult daughter that he could no longer provide with her with a monthly allowance and his brother who worked for him that he could no longer provide him with loans against his salary. This was a huge step and an uncomfortable one for Vincent, but he did it.

Ask yourself, "Who am I becoming by committing to this change?" Vincent still gave a certain amount of money to charities, but he became a person who did not give to friends and relatives when it was clearly obvious he would be disadvantaged by being so generous.

6. Restructure your life to support your decision.

Vincent did this by following a plan to clear all his debt. He took more modest holidays and ate out less. He began to entertain at home more because he still wanted to see his friends, but spent far less.

7. Take the actions you need to support your new life.

Vincent didn't take on any new credit cards. Prior to this, he would take any that were offered. He also stopped seeing so often a particular friend who, Vincent felt, looked down on anyone who didn't have a flashy car. He realised this snobbish type of person was no longer compatible with the new unpretentious person he had become.

Action Steps

Make sure you fully understand the seven steps to changing a money mindset. The steps are:

1. Identify where you are now.
2. Identify what you want in detail.
3. Why do you want it, exactly?
4. Decide to do it and fully commit to the decision.
5. Accept that this means a whole new way of life.
6. Restructure your life to support your decision.
7. Take the actions you need to support your new life.

What actions will you need to take as a direct result of the change you have committed to? Will it mean any changes for the people in your life? How will you deal with this?

Chapter 9

What's Stopping You?

"The opposite of courage in our society is not cowardice.
It is conformity."
Rollo May

Conformity leads us to become incapable of 'thinking outside the box', or worse still, teaches us to create non-existent boxes. We stunt our lives and growth to within the limits of our imaginary confines. There is a story of baby fish that were put in a large tank. One half of the tank was blocked by a big sheet of glass, so they could only swim in the other half. When they had grown to become adult fish, the sheet of glass was taken away. Instead of now using the whole tank, however, the adult fish continued to only use the half that had previously been available to them. They had learned when tiny that a barrier existed, but were unable to adapt to a new reality after that barrier was removed.

There is a similar story about how the mahout trains the baby elephant. A baby elephant is placed on a chain that is staked to the ground. The chain is substantial enough to stop him from pulling it out.

Every time the baby elephant tries to go its own way or break free from its restraints, he can't. He's stuck.

After many attempts, trying and getting nowhere, the little elephant eventually gives up. He believes he can't get away and so stops trying. When the elephant grows to full size, he still thinks the chain is stronger than he is, although he could now easily break free with just one pull. He has learned that being chained means being trapped. The size of the chain is irrelevant. He doesn't even try to break free because he believes he can't.

Learned Helplessness

Learned Helplessness is a term coined by psychologist Dr Martin Seligman who has done groundbreaking research into depression and anxiety. He identified three elements linked to pessimistic thinking: *permanent* - things will always be this way; *pervasive* - I will experience this wherever I am; and *personal* - it's my fault, I'm to blame.

This same process of learned helplessness keeps us humans stuck with results we do not want in our lives.

Like the fish and the elephant, we do not see that the barrier has gone or how easily we could break free. What makes it even harder is that we are often surrounded by people who believe in the same imaginary barriers, all agreeing with each other that these barriers are real, and that someone who tries to break free is wrong, bad, selfish, foolish or all of these things and worse! Rather than be rejected by those we love, we conform – even if that means never living life in a way that is true to ourselves. We are chained and not free to enjoy the experiences we could.

Therefore when we contemplate becoming someone different, we understand that there will be some negative consequences.

People who are part of our lives might not want to come with us. This can be painful and frightening. Such fear can be overwhelming.

Fear stops many of us from leading the lives we want. We fear what other people will think, feel and do if we change. We understand that to be successful we need to operate on a whole different level, but fear others' reactions. We fear not conforming and being different.

Your Financial Neighbourhood

There is a concept called the 'financial neighbourhood', which suggests you earn pretty much the same as your closest family, friends and associates, usually within plus or minus 25%. How do you think your friends and family would think, feel and act if you added two or even three zeros to your annual household income? Do you think things would change?

People who choose to have all the money they want in life have made a choice. To make this choice, you are likely to evolve into someone different from those around you. Your beliefs and values will have to realign. The consequences of committing to this mean you will have to completely change who you are. Of course this is frightening.

Fear of Success

People look at me in disbelief when I say fear of success can stop people having the money they want in life. However when we truly understand success this makes more sense. In order to become successful there are life consequences. You would have to consistently adopt the beliefs, values, feelings, thoughts, decisions and actions of a successful person.

How would that impact your life now if you chose to do

those things? What impact would your decision have on the lives of your family, friends, work colleagues, etc.?

Fear of Failure

This is a very real fear for many. They think: "What if I change everything, take all these huge risks and it doesn't work out? Everybody will tell me they had told me so, or worse."

The truth is, it won't work out in any way as you envisaged. Whenever we jump to the next level and work on new skills we will make mistakes and spend time 'failing' before we figure out how to get it right. The trick is to keep going, keep taking the next small step even when nothing seems to be working and we feel discouraged.

When you commit to making a change in your money mindset you will be choosing success over failure and will learn how to turn things around, even when they don't go according to plan. Every little step you take in the right direction, every little shift in your money mindset over time builds up to a big change and more financial success. You are never a failure when you keep going and working to make the changes you need. You are only a failure if you give up. Like the old saying – *Quitters never win and winners never quit!*

Too Lazy

The reason we don't have the wealth we want in our lives can often be because we are too lazy! By this I mean putting in the hard work to change. You have to confront and blast through whatever is holding you back, which frequently turns out to be what David Neagle calls 'The Excuse': that is the reason/excuse you are using to let yourself off the hook.

For you that might be a lack of education, time, or skills or where you live; in fact anything that you are believing to be a barrier to your financial success. Sustaining the motivation and challenging yourself to do something different is hard work and takes serious gumption. It takes a lot of determination to change your money mindset and to choose to take total responsibility for your financial success. It means focussing your efforts every day on using your existing money with intention and figuring ways to create more.

Other Priorities

Another reason we don't have the financial success we want is we believe other priorities get in the way.

Some will say, "I'd rather be happy than have money;" but this statement is a *Poor* money mindset from someone who is happier without financial success than with challenging themselves. That is absolutely fine, as long as they don't resent their lack of financial success, or others who have pushed themselves to become successful. Sometimes people use the excuse they are too busy to sort their finances or do not have time to look for a new job or start a business. These are excuses, not real reasons. If someone wants to become more financially successful badly enough, they will find a way to make the changes.

Illness, Childcare and Coming from a Poor Background

Caring for others forms a big part of life for some people who care day-to-day for dependents, perhaps children or an elderly relative. Others may not be well themselves.

No matter what is happening, someone can choose to make good or poor decisions with the money they have. They can decide to give up and believe that their financial success is at the mercy of their children, or elderly relative, or their own health, or anything else. In reality, we know of many people who succeeded in tough situations: JK Rowling was a broke single parent; Oprah Winfrey had a very poor and troubled background; Mark Pearson (who founded *MyVoucherCodes.co.uk* and ended up with a company worth $100m) grew up in a council flat in Liverpool.

We make a choice about who we aspire to be, and what we are willing to do to become that person. I wonder how different the world would be if Martin Luther King, Stephen Hawking, Nelson Mandela or the scores of people with the odds firmly stacked against, had just fallen back on their 'Excuse' and chosen never to pursue their ideals.

Action Steps

Spotting What's Stopping You

1. Identify your 'Excuse'. This is the next immediate barrier you see to your financial success.
   For example, *"The market is saturated for the product I'm selling"*; *"I'm no good with numbers"*; *"I don't know what to do."*
   There are as many individual excuses as there are individuals in the world.

2. Working on that barrier is your next step. If your excuse is *"I'm no good at IT"*, or *"selling"*, then you need to work on that.

3. Repeat steps 1 and 2 over and over, tackling a new excuse every time. After a period of time you will be incredibly successful.

Chapter 10

Time is Worth More Than Money

Procrastination Kills Success

That old phrase *"Time is money"* is probably one of the most stupid phrases I have ever heard. Whoever coined that must have had rather a miserable life if they equated their time with mere money. Money cannot buy you another second on this planet once you are dead. This is why procrastination is such an evil – because for every second we waste, we can never get it back; for every second we spend doing something we don't want to, or pretend to be someone or something we are not, we are frittering away the number of moments when we can truly become ourselves and live the life we choose.

Procrastination kills success in its tracks. Every time.

We all have the same amount of time each day. It doesn't matter whether you are Richard Branson, Lady Gaga or … you. Twenty-four hours each day. That's all we have.

One of my favourite insights is that when someone says they don't have time, what they really mean is, *"I am choosing to spend my time on something else"*.

Each of us has 24 hours a day. We get to choose how we spend it.

Bill Gates once said: *"If you're born poor, it's not your mistake. But if you die poor, it is your mistake."*

This provokes several strong reactions. People who regard the poor as victims of the rich find it appalling. And of course there are countless instances worldwide of where the poor are exploited by the rich. However, there are also countless examples of poor people escaping poverty and becoming rich. The only thing these people can do is to use their time like a rich person. If they consistently do this every day, they cannot *not* succeed.

There are enormous inequalities in the world with regard to wealth, education, environmental resources and so on, yet we are all equal when it comes to the matter of time. Taking responsibility for our lives and learning how to make our lives better are the only ways we can take back some power and control.

Time is equal for all. How we use the 24 hours that we have in each day depends on us.

Although many continue to believe in the saying that 'time is money', I do not consider it to be true. Time is everything, so much more important than money. If you lost a million pounds you could get it back. If you waste an hour, no matter how rich you are, you will never get that hour back.

Total determination to succeed will pay off.

A successful person focuses on a goal and pursues it relentlessly.

No matter how many setbacks they go through, they get up, get positive and start again. You will not suddenly become successful when something successful 'happens' to you; something successful will happen for you because you work at being successful every single day.

Not one stroke of luck, but day after day; week after week; month in, month out; year in, year out consistently focussing and taking the right actions will deliver results. Background may well make a difference but, as I observed while growing up, attitudes make a difference too.

My grandparents had very different attitudes. My great grandfather William Roche, whom I introduced earlier, came from a very poor farming background. He loved farming and wanted nothing more than to spend his life as a farmer. However the family farm was given to his older brother.

On the other hand, my maternal grandmother, Mary Wright, came from a wealthy farming background. In her case, the family farm was also given to her brother, Tom, and Granny always felt embittered that it was not divided fairly.

Let's find out what happened to William Roche. He was indentured to a retail company in Cork at the age of 14, living in hideous conditions for nine years.

However, he was an observant lad and while working, noticed that retail goods were targeted towards the wealthier folk in the community. An idea took hold in his mind; he nurtured a dream.

William wanted to set up a large shop that would provide goods for ordinary people, something totally unheard of in Ireland at that time.

He saved every penny for those nine years, then borrowed what he could to open his shop. It failed. He started again and set up another. That too failed. He started yet again. This time, his enterprise became one of the most successful chains of department stores in Ireland in its day, and my great grandfather became extremely wealthy.

Things went rather differently for Mary Wright.

She moved to Limerick and married a poor wood turner. They scraped a living together.

She was an intelligent, nice and funny lady, but developed a resentment and hatred of the rich that lasted all her life. Her good qualities were amazing; when she died we could not believe the people who had been her friends – members of parliament, the clergy, the great and the good. A huge crowd turned up to pay their respects at her funeral. And she deserved it. I noticed that Granny had died utterly penniless, still hating and resenting the rich. She never had a dream to become successful; she just resented those who were.

If you choose to believe that you have no control because of your past, gender, race, upbringing, education, skills or anything else, then you are handing your personal power over to whoever or whatever you think is the reason you cannot succeed. Take your power back! Choose to become who you want to be, and succeed in getting the life you want on your terms.

You will do this by using your most precious resource and by focussing completely on getting the results you want. Getting what you want in life is all about how you use your time. You can tell so much about a person from how they use their time.

Time and Energy

Where your energy goes, the results flow. The results you see in your life are all about how you use your time.

Think about it – how do you believe people spend their time differently when you take into account their money mindset?

People of the various mindsets spend time the way they spend money. Those with a *Rich* money mindset tend to spend their time where it will give them the best return.

Making new contacts/connections, learning new things, getting out of their comfort zone. They tend not to spend time procrastinating, complaining, or watching lots of television. However, those with in-debt, break-even and even comfortable mindsets may be more likely to stay in their comfort zone for long periods of time, and even spend long periods on activities with very little added value.

Exercise
Who Does What?

To gain an understanding of these differences, complete the exercise below.

Look at the list of activities in *Appendix 4* and tick the ones you think someone with a particular money mindset would use their time.

Change Your Use of Time, Change Your Life

Where you spend your time determines the outcomes in your life. It makes sense then that changing your life starts with changing how you spend your time. This is of course easier said than done. It means completely changing how you 'spend' your life, in other words, what you do in the time you have. Ultimately, it means changing deep-down beliefs and habits.

Become the Change

As change expert, neuroscientist and author Dr. Joe Dispenza, says, you need to completely let go of the habit of being yourself.

To get the level of choice and freedom you want in your life, you have to become that person internally. You are the one who has made the choices that have created your life and finances.

If you knew how to make different choices, you would have. The only way you can get things to change around you is to change yourself!

How to make a successful change

The first thing in making a successful change is desire. What do you want more than anything in your life? What matters to you more than anything? For me it was to be able to choose what I do every day. This meant everything to me. I like my own time and space. I like to create. I like to feel free; to go where I want, when I want. to live where I want and how I want.

I hate the constraints of a job. I love sitting in a wreck of a property envisioning how to make it magnificent. That fills me with unbounded joy and when I see the building come to life again, I just love it! When I teach people that they can do the same with their lives and choose to do what they enjoy above all else, I love it! I love it when the penny drops for someone and they learn something totally new, which means they can live life more on their terms, and can say: *"Lots of people might not agree with my choices, but I don't care. I'm happy now."*

Ask yourself the question: *"If money was no object, what would I do?"* The answer will be very informative for you. What would you do today, this week, this month, this year, in five years, in 10 years, if you had all the money you could spend? If the answers are very different to the life you are living now, you need to make some big changes. You owe it to yourself to live the life you dream of.

Money makes you more of what you are

Some say more money doesn't change you; it just makes you more of what you are. If you had limitless money, you would be more of what you are - your core values.

To create wealth, you will need to be more of what you are, because in this lies your passion. If you are doing something in your life that makes you less of what you are or can be, you will find it impossible to live life to the fullest. Your precious time and your life are being wasted.

I knew a lady whose heart's desire was to be free. She was married to someone who hated change but she was driven to feel free, to get up and go, and to live wherever she fancied!

Clearly this was a incompatible partnership with each making the other miserable. The couple had become quite wealthy but for the one who hated change, the wealth provided the power to keep things the same; while for the one who craved continual change, the wealth opened up a world of possibilities. In the end each went their separate ways and created the different lives they wanted.

Once you understand your life's desire, get really specific about exactly what it is you want.

For me, in my property business, that means getting to the point where I can visualise the property I am going to buy, and the exact figures that will make the deal work.

At this level of detail you have direction. 'Direction' is your aim and your strategy, how you will get to your destination. Brendan Burchard, author and motivational speaker, says you need to "chase down your how." Model how others who have done what you want to do, have done it. Stretch your competency – commit to becoming the best in your chosen field. He talks about the need for gathering information, knowledge and wisdom.

In Montana, where he comes from, there is a saying: *"The time to have the map is before you enter the woods."*

To achieve this, you need daily habits. You will need the discipline to put in the work to become the person willing to learn new stuff.

You need dogged persistence, every day doing a bit towards your vision. Decide on having an unswerving commitment to attaining your vision. As Joe Dispenza says, you need to change yourself to become the person who can achieve these goals.

You must also develop a finely tuned *Distraction Radar* to bring into your awareness every distraction that enters your life that could potentially kill your life's desire. Every distraction takes you away from becoming the person you want to be. Every time you allow yourself to become enmeshed in a distraction, you are moving away from the life you should be leading. You can achieve the life you want, but you must commit to do what it takes. For example, when I was developing *The 4 Money Mindsets* and writing this book, I was offered a part-time, temporary job in a company I'd worked in previously. This was the best job I'd ever had. I loved the job itself, my colleagues and that workplace. It took great strength to say no to working for a few days a week for three months. It was a distraction that would devour my time and take me away from my life's work.

Action Steps

Breaking Through

1. Where do you procrastinate? Look at the link between this and your success.

2. Look at someone who is very focussed – ask them how they do it. Follow up their replies with the question "Why is that important?" You will be amazed at how much you learn from applying and imitating the strategy of someone who excels.

Chapter 11

How to Stick to Your New Money Mindset

Going through all the new steps to mindset change is a process that is both challenging and rewarding. However, all will come to nothing unless you work in your new mindset every day. Consistency is key.

In this chapter we will look at tools and techniques to support consistent practice of your new mindset.

Develop Good Habits

Where you are in life and everything you have achieved so far is an accumulation of the results of your daily habits. If you do the same thing over and over, either positive or negative, it will produce results. Setting a goal is fine, but if you don't do a bit towards that goal every day you will never reach it.

Action is everything, even if you take only the tiniest step in the right direction. Small daily actions with regard to money will accumulate into big results.

The Kumon Learning system for children is a wonderful example of the power of achievement through habits.

This system, invented by a Japanese educationalist and entrepreneur, is followed by young children after school, all over the world.

The pupil does a number of study questions on maths, English or Japanese every day, seven days a week, 12 months a year. My little girl was doing approximately 50 maths questions a day totalling 18,000 maths questions a year through this system. She began when she was five and is now nine. During that time she has totalled 75,000 basic maths questions. Teachers at school comment on how brilliant she is at maths. It's hardly surprising. This is a great example of the power of daily habits.

To reach your goal, the key is to do a little bit every day. Develop the habit of having an unswerving commitment to doing something, no matter how little, to take you closer to your goal every day.

Money Habits

Good money habits are critical to financial success. Practiced over and over, they lead to big results. What might happen if you got into the habit of checking your current account every single morning? If you did this without fail you would probably find that you have more money. Why? Because the habit of checking makes you more conscious of frivolous and unplanned expenditure.

A habit of carrying cash instead of cards leads you to spend only what you have, and not unconsciously exceed your spending limit. A habit of saving just £1 a day (£365 a year) in a bank with compound interest at a rate of 3% would give you £10,731.67 after 20 years for very little effort.

Can you imagine the effect of habitually applying a new, positive, financial behaviour for the next 10 years? For example, saving a specific amount every payday before doing anything else with your money? Or consistently paying all your bills first before spending anything?

Or leveraging some of your money to make more, every time your profits come in? Can you imagine what might happen if you did any of these actions as rigorously as my daughter did four years of Kumon maths! Without doubt, you would have formed a habit of whatever mindset you chose – and reaped the rewards.

Some of my clients find that keeping a log of their spending is revealing. In fact, it provides a good starting point for money habits they want to change.

Keeping a Spending Log

For at least one month, make a detailed note of every single penny you spend. Keep all your receipts and write the expenses down regularly. Be sure you record even the smallest expenditures because these really reveal a lot about what you use your money for. Guaranteed!

Also, those with the least controlled spending habits seem to be most liable to forget what they have spent within minutes of spending.

One of my clients who ran a deep *In-debt* mindset was completely convinced that either she had lost a significant amount of money or someone had stolen it.

She had, of course, spent it!

You could also keep a similar log for how you use your time – making a note of the specific actions you take every day to analyse how you are spending your time.

Monthly Spending Log

See *Appendix 1* for instructions and a template for keeping a spending log.

When you have a log for a full month, review your list and everything you have spent at the end of that month. What patterns do you see? Look specifically at the flow of your money. Where does it flow to? What do your purchases give you?

- Do you use every penny as a tool, with intention, to provide something greater for you? Do you use your money as part of a plan to achieve a greater goal?
  Or do you spend to make yourself feel better?
  Do you give to someone or something that is not truly benefitting you or them?

- Are you spending on items that are not necessary?

- Do you treat your money with respect, and consider the value/return you are getting each time you use it, or do you simply spend and avoid even thinking about it?

- Do you yearn for things and think you can't afford them, rather than working out how you can afford them?

The spending log will give you a clearer view of where your money is going. You might even see that sometimes you spend without purpose; that you are not using money as a tool to enhance your life but spending without understanding the consequences.

The Money Matrix

A key to financial success is to properly understand 'the flow of money'. I developed the money matrix (see *Appendix 2*) for my clients as a way of helping them to understand the concept of the 'flow of money' and apply it to their personal money flow.

This shows how the amount of money you currently have in your control is not the critical factor in your future financial success, but how you make your existing wealth flow. It shows how our money flows in and out; and whether wealth will ever flow to us and increase, or always flow away from us.

Money flows to us in two ways:

- *From a 'Bonus'* – Money can flow to you on a 'one-off basis', that is *Bonus Money*, such as winnings, a redundancy payment, a bonus at work, inheritance and so on – anything that is beyond your control and thus hard to replicate and scale up.

- *From a 'Wealth Producer'* – Money can flow to you from *Wealth Producers*, which are systems you have created to produce money for you. For example, investments, businesses, royalties, property, etc.
  The more of these you create, the more money you can produce for yourself. *Wealth Producers* can be small, supplying you with little chunks of money; or you can grow them to produce much more.

Money flows from us in three directions:

- *It flows away on 'Wealth Takers'.* You can use money to buy Wealth Takers – your house, your car, holidays, etc. A Wealth Taker is anything you do or own that takes money out of your pocket.

- *It can flow to a 'Dead End'.* Here, it languishes, and can lose its value and die. This is what happens if you hoard money; I call it *'Dead Wealth'.* For example, hoarding much more that the required emergency fund and six months' living expenses as savings. If you save/hoard money, it will not work hard for you and dwindle in value over time.

- It can flow to create more through creating a *'Wealth Producer'* system. The more of these you create, the more money you can produce. Doing this will mean building the habits of the *Rich* money mindset, day after day until you get to a point where your *Wealth Producers* provide 100% of your cash flow and generate further money to reinvest in *Wealth Producers.* Then, in terms of growing your wealth, the sky is the limit.

How does your money flow?

Look at your expenditure log and categorise the flow and expenses using the *Money Matrix.* How is it flowing? Does it flow freely from *Wealth Producers* or are you reliant on a Bonus? Maybe you are even living from Bonus to Bonus?

When it comes in, what exactly are you doing with the extra cash? Are you using your money to achieve your goals? Do your money habits support the results you have seen over the long term? Or do you need to use your money differently? Do you want to set some high level goals? If you want a raft of *Wealth Producers,* such goals will require you study a little bit every day to learn how to build them.

Great success and achieving your goals is all about the little things you do. Introduce better daily habits around money and shift your money mindset to make a big difference over time.

The People Around You

There is an old adage: "You are the average of the five people you spend most time with." Who you spend time with matters hugely because you take on the norms of your group. If you want to change your mindset around money you must spend time with those who have the mindset you want. Look at the people you spend most of the time with: what are their financial lives like and what is their money mindset? Do you want the financial results they have? If not, go out and find some people who have the results you aspire to and spend time with them. You will be surprised at how quickly you notice shifts in your mindset and financial success.

Use Your Time Wisely

How you use your time directly correlates with the results that show up in your life. In a similar way, how you use your money directly correlates with the amount of wealth you have (or do not have) in your life.

Compare someone who spends their time and money learning to be brilliant at a skill, with another who spends their time and money to impress other people. Which of these people do you suppose will be wealthier and more successful? The first, of course, since those who are trying to be something for the sake of others rather than following their own dreams are rarely successful.

Weekly Time Log

Completing a time log (see *Appendix 3*), like the money log can be invaluable.

In this exercise, make a detailed note of what you do with all of your time over a week. Write down what you have done with your time every hour for one week. Unlike the spending log, you cannot keep receipts on how you have used your time so you will need to write down your activities hourly. If you leave it until the end of the day you'll forget where your time goes. Don't assume you will remember. We seem to forget our biggest time wasters! I know this exercise seems like a pain but the results could inspire you to change your life!

Once you have collated your information, complete the time matrix below.

Completing the time log will give you a clearer view of where your time is going. You might even feel that you sometimes spend your time without purpose, not using it as your most precious resource but squandering it without really understanding the consequences.

The Time Matrix

I developed the time matrix (see *Appendix 4*) with my clients as a way of helping them to understand what is really happening when they use/spend time. This matrix divides time uses into four categories:

- *Time Wasters:* anything that gives you no return.

- *Bonus Time:* time spent on an activity that gives you a one-off return, or a one-off opportunity to gain something positive. For example, earning or having a good time.

- *Dead Time:* time spent in getting some return, either financial or personal, but is not in any way moving you towards your dream. An example of this could be a job or a relationship/ friendship that you know you should let go of, but are avoiding dealing with.

- *Life time:* this is the time you use to build your dream. Learning, making connections, planning, taking each step to achieve your goals. If you give your time to building the habit of the *Rich* money mindset, day after day, you will get to a point where your *Wealth Producers* provide 100% of your cash flow, and generate further money to reinvest in *Wealth Producers*.

To complete the time matrix, total the number of hours on the activities in each category. For example:

- *Time Wasters*, such as television, internet surfing, idling on social media, etc.

- Bonus Time, the activities that have a one-off benefit, such as a piece of consultancy work that yields a one-off payment but no other benefit, or learning something that does not directly align with your end dream. Having a good time also fits into this category.

- Dead Time, hours that you feel obliged to spend on an activity but are not growing your wealth or your life's mission. For example, a job you don't love, or anything in life that you do, but don't love doing.

- Life Time, the activities where your life's passion is ignited, you are learning and building your future. These take you closer to your life's mission.

Money follows your energy and time. If the flow of time or money is towards wasting rather than building, it makes sense that your end results will be very little. If you never spend your time developing the money mindset you want, you will never have the money you want in your life.

Strive for the Next Level

To achieve and maintain lifelong mindset shift, you must commit to lifelong learning. Consistently seek out those who have done what you want to do. Get a mentor or hire a coach who has achieved what you aspire to. Your mentor and coach can help you step by step.

Get out and deliberately meet people who are doing inspiring, innovative work. Make it a habit. It's worth spending on education that you helps you achieve the result you want. Many fear they will be ripped off and you will be if you don't take the time to teach yourself the skills to discern who can genuinely help you and who cannot. Learn, learn, learn.

This means consistently stepping out of your comfort zone. Consistently letting go of the past and old skills in favour of developing the next level up. I have lost count of the number of people I meet who leave the corporate world in midlife and set up businesses that limp along for years producing little income compared to the pay they enjoyed from their corporate job. They don't understand they need to shift from an employee to a business-builder mindset. Many hoard their redundancy payout for fear they will not be able to make it back if they invest and live in self-imposed poverty instead of focussing on gaining the new skillset they need.

"You don't stop learning when you grow old;
you grow old when you stop learning."

Let Go to Grow

This is critical to getting to the next level. You must learn to let go of the successes you had at a mediocre level to jump to the next level. This is a step that really frightens many people. One of my clients is a lovely and caring woman. She likes to be liked and appreciated and has made a successful living as a self-employed beautician. However, when she was ready to launch her own line of products and build the business, she found it very difficult. She now spent much of her time out of her comfort zone, making strategic decisions about branding, marketing and production; but she kept on allowing herself to waste her time by getting sucked into doing treatments for clients who gave her positive feedback. To be successful, she had to let go of this need to be liked, which was destroying her fledgling business because it wasted her time.

In advancing to the next level, a key fear is letting go of the good things you have now when you can't see any guarantee of the good things at the next level. This fear is completely natural, but it's important not to let your trepidation stop you. You may find functioning at a higher level overwhelming at first. You have to learn 'how to' step-by-step. Once you experience success, you build the confidence to know you can create wealth. When you work on this consistently, then you have a *Rich* money mindset. I battled with this in my own businesses, being afraid to invest the necessary money. When I stepped up and viewed the challenges as an entrepreneur, with a *Rich* money mindset, success came.

Be Prepared to Fail

You will fail repeatedly if you have the courage to try new ventures. Our educational system seems designed to hinder success. We are taught that failure is bad and there is a right and wrong answer to any question. This is the opposite of a *Rich* money mindset.

Failures are only failures if you don't learn from them. You will get to a better level because you have tried. You cannot learn and grow if you do not try new skills.

I tell my daughter that the mark of a successful person is someone who willingly tries new things, even though they know it means they will fail lots of times before they get it right.

Consider the Wright Brothers' numerous attempts to build a plane and Edison's 99,999 attempts before getting the light bulb to work. Edison said he did not fail 99,999 times, but learned 99,999 different ways that it did not work. Each time he was getting closer to the solution.

"There is no failure, only feedback."

Reinvent Yourself – Again and Again

Any time you want to change your life, you have the power to do so. Have the courage to reinvent yourself again and again. Reinvention is just mindset change so you can create the life that you want.

Consider applying the 'three strikes and you are out' rule to complaining about things in your life. It works like this – if you find yourself complaining about something once, take note; if you complain about the same thing again, take notice; if you complain about the same thing a third time, either shut up and accept that living with it is your choice, take action and do something about it!

When I look back over the past 12 years I feel enormous gratitude to that part of myself that spurred me to leave behind a life that would never fulfil me, to move away and completely change everything. Or did I completely change and then move away? I think the latter.

Maybe it's chicken and egg syndrome, but one thing is sure, if you want a better life, the time to make the change is now!

Action Steps

Improve Your Habits

1. Complete a spending log.
2. Complete the Money Matrix.
3. Complete a time log.
4. Complete the Time Matrix.
5. Take Action!

Appendix 1: The Spending Log

Monday	Tuesday	Wednesday	Thursday	Friday	Saturday	Sunday
What/ How much?	*What/ How much?*	*What/ How much?*	*What/ How much?*	*What/ How much?*	*What/ How much?*	*What/ How much?*

Appendix 2: The Money Matrix

Wealth Takers	A Bonus	Dead Wealth	Wealth Producers
Rent/Mortgage on house your live in	Salary (you cannot guarantee it, or scale it)	Savings without purpose (more than emergency fund and six months' living expenses)	Business (scalable assets)
Car	Self-employment (selling time for money)	Excessive equity in property	Investments
All consumer debt	Winnings - Lottery/shares	Excessive equity in business	Property
Children	Selling one-off items		Royalties and Patents
Anything that takes money from you	Inheritance		

Appendix 3: The Weekly Time Log

List what you do every hour

Time	Mon	Tue	Wed	Thur	Fri	Sat	Sun
5am							
6am							
7am							
8am							
9am							
10am							
11am							
12							
1pm							
2pm							
3pm							
4pm							
5pm							
6pm							
7pm							
8pm							
9pm							
10pm							
11pm							
12mn							
1am							

Appendix 4: The Time Matrix

Time Wasters	Bonus Time	Dead Time	Time/wealth Producers
Television	Time with friends/family	Dead End job you hate	Learning
Tech (Video games)	Enjoying Yourself	Dead end friendships or relationship/s	Taking action out of your comfort zone
Social Media		In comfort zone	Producing wealth generating products

References

- Bennett, Sophie. (2013). *Money Bondage*. The Wealth Network Ltd.
- Bandler, Richard. (2008). *Get the Life You Want*. HarperElement
- Bodenhamer, Bob, and Hall, L Micheal. (1999). *The User's Manual for the Brain*. Crown House Publishing Ltd.
- Burchard, Brendon. (2011). *The Millionaire Messenger*. Free Press.
- Clason, George, S. (1926). *The Richest Man in Babylon*. Hawthorn/Dutton.
- Dale, Margaret & Iles, Paul. (1992). *Assessing Management Skills*. Kogan Page.
- Dispenza, Dr. Jo. (2012). *Breaking the Habit of Being Yourself: How to lose your mind and create a new one*. Hay House UK.
- Duhigg, Charles. (2012). *The Power of Habit*. Random House.
- Dweck, Carol S. (2012). *Mindset: How you can fulfil your Potential*. Ballentine Books.
- Economist, The. (2014). T*he Economist Numbers Guide. (6th Ed) The Essentials of Business Numeracy*. The Economist Books Ltd.
- Eker, T. Harv. (2005). *Secrets of the Millionaire Mind*. HarperCollins Publishers Inc.

- Dennis, Felix. (2007). *How to Get Rich*. Ebury Press.
- Getty, J. Paul. (1965). *How to be Rich*. Jove Books.
- Godin, Seth. (2015) *What to do when it's your Turn*.
- Graham, Benjamin. (1973). *The intelligent Investor*. Harper & Row.
- Gray, Bernard. (1991). *The Beginners Guide to Investment*. Century Business.
- Gough, Leo. (1996). *(Teach yourself) Savings and Investments*. Hodder and Stoughton Ltd.
- Gunther, Max. (1985). *The Zurich Axioms*. Dutton Plume.
- Hansen, Mark, Victor & Allen, Robert. (2005). *Cracking the Millionaire Code*. Harmony Books.
- Hall, L. Micheal & Charvet, Shelle Rose. (2011). *Innovations in NLP for Challenging Times*. Crown House Publishing Ltd.
- Hall, L. Micheal. (2002). *The Matrix Model: The 7 Matrices of Neuro Semantics*. Neuro-Semantics Publications.
- Hill, Napoleon. (2007) *Master Keys to Riches*. Vermillion
- Holt, Jon & Perry Simon, A. (2011). *A Pragmatic Guide to Competency: Tools, Frameworks and Assessment*. British Informatics Society Limited.
- Karpman, Dr Steven B. MD. (1967). *The Karpman Drama Triangle*, in Byrne, E. M.D. (2016). *Games People Play, The Psychology of Human Relationships*. Pengiun Life.
- Klontz, Brad. Kahler, Rick & Klontz, Ted. (2008). *Facilitating Financial Health*. The National Underwriter Company.
- Klontz, Brad. Kahler, Rick & Klontz, Ted. (2008). *Wired for Wealth*. Health Communications Inc.
- Klontz, Brad & Klontz, Ted. (2009) *Mind over Money*. Broadway Books. Random House, New York.
- Kiyosaki, T. Robert. (2009). *Rich Dad's Conspiracy of the Rich*. Businesses Plus, Hachette Book Group.

- Kiyosaki, T. Robert. & Lechter, Sharon L. (2004). *Who took my Money?* Warner Business Books.
- Lewis, Martin. (2005). *The Money Diet.* Vermillion
- Levine, Tony. (2004). *Investing for Dummies.* John Wiley and Sons, Ltd.
- Liddy, Pat & Roche, Stanley. (2006). *William Roche 1874 – 1939, The Story of William Roche and The Founding of Roches Stores.* Published privately.
- Maloney, Michael. (2008). *Guide to Investing in Gold and Silver. Business Plus.* Hachette Publishing.
- McConnell, Carmel. (2005). *Make Money Be Happy.* Pearson Education Limited.
- Nemeth, Maria. (1977). *The Energy of Money.* Ballentine Wellspring.
- Neagle, David. (2013). *The Millions Within.* Morgan James Publishing.
- Orman, Suze, (2005). *The Laws of Money.* Simon & Schuster UK Ltd.
- Priestley, Andrew. (2016). *The Money Chimp.* Writing Matters Publishing.
- Prochanska. James, O. et al. (1994). *Changing For Good.* Collins Living.
- Seligman, Martin. (2006) *Learned Optimism.* Vintage Books USA.

About the Author

Karen Sutton-Johal is a Learning and Skills specialist, debt advisor and financial success coach, who has spent 12 years helping people understand how their money mindset determines their financial success.

Her fascination with money was sparked when, as a child her father's business collapsed. She keenly observed how people's attitudes to money caused vastly different financial results in their lives.

Her academic and professional experience allowed her to delve deeper into understanding people's relationship with money. Her background includes corporate executive coaching, leadership and management training, an MA in Human Resources Management, qualifications in Ability Testing and Personality Profiling from the British Psychological Society and qualifying as an NLP Master Practitioner. Her work as a debt adviser led her to discover 'The 4 Money Mindsets'

Building a successful social housing business with her husband Jo, over a decade, resulted in them becoming financially free in 2012. This experience contributed to her understanding of what it takes to develop the *Rich Money Mindset.*

She and her husband run the *Personal Money Mindshift, Business Money Mindshift* and *Rich Money Mindset Mastermind* workshops. They offer individual coaching which transform clients' finances.

She lives in the beautiful Peak District with her husband and daughter.

Contacts

- Facebook
  http://www.facebook.com/ThePennydrops1/

- Linkedin
  https://www.linkedin.com/in/karensuttonjohal/en

- Twitter
  http://twitter.com/ThePennyDrops_

- Website
  http://www.the4moneymindsets.com

  Email
- Karen@the4moneymindsets.com